ACE VERSUS ACE!

The highest-scoring German ace to survive World War I, Ernst Udets, describes his aerial meeting with Georges Guynemer, the almost supernaturally skilled French air fighter:

"At the same height, we go for each other, passing at a hair's breadth. We bank into a left turn. The other's aircraft shines brown in the sun. Sometimes we pass so closely I can clearly recognize a narrow, pale face under the leather helmet. On the leather fuselage, between the wings, there is a word in black letters. As he passes me for the fifth time, so close that the propwash shakes me back and forth, I can make it out: *"Vieux"* it says there...Yes, only one man flies like this on our front: that's Guynemer's sign.

"I do a half loop in order to come down on him from above. He understands at once, and also starts a loop. I try anything I can, tightest banks, turns, sideslips, but with lightning speed, he anticipates all my moves and reacts at once. Slowly I realize his superiority. His aircraft is better, he can do more than I, but I continue to flght. Once out of the turn, he can get me in his sights for a moment. Metallic hail rattles through my right wing and rings out as it hits the struts..."

THE
ACE FACTOR

MIKE SPICK

AVON BOOKS ▲ NEW YORK

The Naval Institute Press is the book-publishing arm of the U.S. Naval Institute, a private, nonprofit professional society for members of the sea services and civilians who share an interest in naval and maritime affairs. Established in 1873 at the U.S. Naval Academy in Annapolis, Maryland, where its offices remain today, the Naval Institute has more than 100,000 members worldwide.

U.S. hardcover edition published by The Naval Institute Press, Annapolis, Maryland; original hardcover edition published in England by Airlife Publishing Ltd., 7 St. John's Hill, Shrewsbury.

AVON BOOKS
A division of
The Hearst Corporation
105 Madison Avenue
New York, New York 10016

Copyright © 1988 by Mike Spick
Pubished by arrangement with Naval Institute Press
Library of Congress Catalog Card Number: 88-61704
ISBN: 0-380-70825-6

First Avon Books Printing: November 1989

AVON TRADEMARK REG. U.S. PAT. OFF. AND IN OTHER COUNTRIES, MARCA REGISTRADA, HECHO EN U.S.A.

Printed in the U.S.A.

OPM   10   9   8   7   6   5   4   3   2   1

Contents

Nine-tenths of tactics were certain enough to be teachable in schools; but the irrational tenth was like the kingfisher flashing across the pool, and in it lay the test of generals.

—Colonel T. E. Lawrence,
Seven Pillars of Wisdom, Book III

and fighter pilots!

—Major T. E. Lorincz, USAF.

Acknowledgments

While I am solely responsible for the opinions expressed herein, and the conclusions drawn, this book is but the tip of the iceberg. Invisible beneath it are many first hand accounts, both published and unpublished, and many learned papers which I might never have heard of, had it not been for the assistance of the following: Roy A. Grossnick of the USN Naval Aviation History and Archives, William C. Heimdahl of the USAF Office of Air Force History, Mr. Brian Cocks, Robert Shackleton Blake of McDonnell Douglas, Shlomo Kleszcelski, Colonel Reade Tilley USAF (ret), Lieutenant Colonel William D. Lafever USAF (ret), and Major Thomas E. Lorincz USAF. I am also indebted to Blake Morrison, Editor of *USAF Fighter Weapons Review,* for permission to print large extracts from *No Guts, No Glory,* by Major General Frederick C. Blesse USAF (ret), which for many years was the fighter pilot's "bible."

The transcript of the interview with Captain David McCampbell USN (ret), by Paul Stillwell, July 1987, reproduced by kind permission of the United States Naval Institute Press.

THE
ACE FACTOR

Introduction

Since the dawn of history, man has shown a propensity for armed conflict. In every age, a few men have emerged as being outstandingly good at war, and their names have been handed down to posterity. Most of them have been commanders and generals, such as Alexander the Great, Hannibal, Alfred the Great, Richard Coeur de Lion, Henry V, Bertrand du Guesclin, Gustavus Adolphus, Napoleon and Nelson. Others, and they have been fewer, for obvious reasons, have made their reputations at a lower level. Names that spring to mind are William Marshall, the medieval English champion, Yasotay, the foremost warrior of Ghengis Khan's Golden Horde who was never promoted as it might have ruined his fighting qualities, Miyamoto Musashi, the Samurai, who triumphed in over sixty individual combats, and Lifeguardsman Shaw, who cut down nine French cuirassiers at Waterloo before falling himself.

As the years passed, armies grew progressively larger and conscription became the norm. Weaponry grew ever more long-ranged and devastating, and men were herded into battle like cattle to the slaughter, with little chance to show their prowess before they were mown down at a distance too far for their executioners to even see what they looked like. This inhuman process reached its peak on the Western Front during the First World War, where huge armies, well dug in, faced each other across a few hundred yards of shell-torn ground, cowering from the monumental artillery barrages put up by both sides, with little or no chance of hitting back. When an attack was launched, the infantry were mown down by nests of concealed machine guns. Glory had a hollow ring in these surroundings of mass slaughter and mud.

High above the ruined landscape, away from the mass murder, the mud, and the reek of the battlefield, a new form of warfare had begun. Man, ever inventive, had taken to the air, and as is usual with every technical advance, had adapted it as a means of killing his fellows. In later years, air warfare was to grow hideous, striking indiscriminately at combatants and non-combatants alike, but to the infantryman at the time, up to his ankles in water, sharing his cold dugout with rats, and seeing his friends torn to pieces by high explosive shells fired with cold impartiality from many miles away, it was a new world. Fighting in the air was clean, exciting and glamorous; it smacked more of the chivalry of old; it was individual combat with man against man, machine against machine. Death, when it came, was quick and very personal, even spectacular. War pilots became the new knights, who could reckon up their individual victories, unlike the average artilleryman who, although he may easily have killed far more of the enemy, never knew it.

In many ways the wheel has turned full circle. War in the air has become more impersonal that it ever could have been in those early days. Now, over seventy years later, the fighter pilot is a highly trained technician rather than a knight, able to launch homing missiles at a target which is only seen as a tiny flicker on a radar screen. On the other hand, this is not always the case, and he must be prepared to oppose the enemy face to face and at close quarters, just as his grandfathers did in the skies above Flanders.

It is a truism of air combat that every victory demands a victim. What is truly surprising is that in every air war fought to date, a tiny minority run up a high score, primarily at the expense of the less gifted. These are the aces, about five percent of the total number of fighter pilots, who historically have accounted for roughly forty percent of the total victories claimed. By general, although not necessarily official definition, an ace is a pilot who has scored five or more victories. Many fighter pilots have scored four or five times this number: some have racked up ten times more, while the world's ranking fighter ace is Erich Hartmann of the Luftwaffe, who scored a total of 352 victories in the Second World War.

The question has often been asked: what particular quality or qualities was it that set these men apart from their peers? Was it simply the possession of a better airplane, or superior marksmanship? Were they better led, or better trained? Did they possess greater flying skills than the average, or could they have merely been luckier? The only thing that is certain is that they were very determined, and generally had excellent distance vision. Or was it that they had all of these qualities in fuller measure than the average? Let us examine all these points in turn.

A better airplane than that flown by the opponent is undoubtedly an advantage, but the record shows that there have been many instances down the years where a seemingly outclassed airplane, not necessarily even a fighter, has emerged victorious over an apparently very superior opponent. Nor is numerical superiority in the engagement a guarantee of success, although on plenty of occasions it has helped. Marksmanship is a different matter; almost all the higher scoring aces have been marksmen, although shooting ability or the lack of it has often meant the difference between a low and a high scoring ace. On the other hand, not all marksmen have become aces, usually because they didn't live long enough. In the current missile age, marksmanship has lost much of its value, although it can always be argued that shooting ability of a different nature is required.

High quality training helps to a degree, as it enables the pilot to get the utmost out of his machine and its weapons. On the other hand, the record shows that many extremely well-trained pilots do not survive their first few encounters with the enemy. Leadership seems to have a far greater effect, and it is particularly noticeable that certain units, of whatever period, have produced more than their share of high scorers. It also keeps the novice out of disadvantageous situations until he has gained experience. Superior flying skills are also an advantage, although aerobatic artists have rarely become aces and test pilots never, although not a few fighter aces have later become test pilots. Many aces have been described as only average aircraft handlers, although naturally this is a subjective judgement. This myth, for myth it surely is, probably stems from the fact that most successful fighter pilots were men of first class judgement, which enabled them in the main to avoid situations where their superior flying skills were called for, with the result that their flying often seemed to lack *élan*. Of course, they may not have been above average flyers at the outset, but improved with practice. Another reason for this myth may be that many of the well-publicized aces of the First World War piled up their aircraft on landing. But so did everybody else, and while Fred Bloggs could do it without the fact being recorded for posterity, if the Red Baron did it, it was sure to be widely known.

The most indefinable quality of all is luck, chance, call it what you will. Very few of the top-scoring fighter pilots of any era avoided being shot down, often more than once. Often bullets missed their bodies by inches, still more frequently their aircraft were well ventilated, but they survived. They were not immortal; quite a high percentage of them were killed in the long run, but without an element of luck at some point they would not have survived as long as they did, and their deeds would have been correspondingly less. Luck is essentially a defensive quality linked with survival, and much less a factor in the attack. Modern United States Navy fighter pilots have a saying, "I'd rather be lucky than good any day."

Determination is an essential part of the make-up of a successful fighter pilot, without which he is unable to function effectively. Many fighter aces have been described as fearless; this is simply not true. What they have to do is to control their fear, which demands a high degree of determination. Determination should not, of course, be confused with aggression: aggression is a double-headed axe, and unless it is used in a cool and calculating manner, can prove lethal to the user. The "fangs out, hair on fire" character may get results for a short while, but sooner or later inevitably gets himself into a situation from which there is no exit.

Of the physical qualities required, good distance vision and good co-ordination are essential. The ability to see small objects at a great distance is paramount, and successful fighter pilots are almost invariably long sighted. Anyone who doubts this should visit a veterans' reunion; the number of pairs of half-moon spectacles or bifocals on display is truly amazing. To digress for a moment, during the summer of 1986 the author attended an American squadron reunion where two distinguished flyers of high rank, both veterans of South-East Asia, solemnly debated the merits of blue or brown eyes. It is an odd fact that about eighty percent of all fighter aces have either blue or light colored eyes! It is an equally odd fact that most fighter aces are on the short side, although there are enough exceptions to prove the rule. As the saying goes, fighter jocks are little guys with big wrist watches! Even more odd, they tend to have more daughters than sons!

Ideally a fighter unit should be manned entirely by aces, but in times of peace it has proved impossible to pick out the potential high scorers, while in war there are never enough to go around. From the foregoing, we can build up a composite picture; a long-sighted young man with light colored eyes, on the short side, with good physical co-ordination, quick reflexes, and a naturally good shot. He should be determined and aggressive, but self-disciplined, with a flair for flying. He can then be given the best possible training and mounted in a first class fighter. The trouble is that thousands upon thousands of young men fitting this description, from many nations, have down the years, strapped a fighter onto their backs and gone forth to battle, never to return. Many of those who do return go out again and again, but achieve little. The gulf between the average fighter pilot and the successful one is very wide. In fact, it is arguable that there are almost *no* average fighter pilots; just aces and turkeys; killers and victims. American analyst Herbert K. Weiss published an article called "Systems Analysis Problems of Limited War" in 1966. He concluded that only one pilot in every fifteen has a better than even chance of surviving his first decisive combat, but having done so, after five such encounters, his survival probability had increased by a factor of *twenty*. The data used to formulate this hypothesis was limited in scope, being derived from three sources. These were the records of *Jagdgeschwader 1*, the *Escadrille Lafayette*, and the records of American flyers serving with other French units, all in World War 1; and the records of *Jagdgeschwader 26* in World War 2. While not very wide ranging, it accords very well with the statistic that only about five percent of fighter pilots become aces, and supports the unarguable fact that this tiny minority tends to

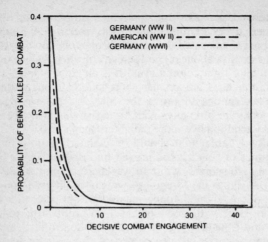

This figure, drawn from the Herbert K. Weiss study of 1966, plots the probability of being killed against the number of decisive engagements. As Weiss himself commented, "the almost vertical drop in probability in the first five decisive combats was totally unexpected." The inference is that some special quality, unrelated to flying experience, is at work.

run up large scores at the expense of the less gifted majority.

We know that it happens; but why? Some mysterious ingredient appears to exist in the few, and if this could only be identified, the whole business of selecting fighter pilots would be revolutionized. Only in the early years of the 1980s does it seem to have been identified with sufficient accuracy to be named. It is Situational Awareness; SA for short, and commonly referred to as "the Clue Bird."

SA is a combination of many things, but in essence it is the ability of the pilot to keep track of events and foresee occurrences in the fast-moving, dynamic scenario of air warfare. Major John R. Boyd, USAF, in an August 1976 briefing called "New Conception for Air to Air Combat" stated "He who can handle the quickest rate of change survives." This was one of the final clues to SA, which even yet defies precise quantification. SA has no relationship to either flying ability or experience in its purest sense, although at a practical level the right sort of experience helps. SA is the Ace Factor; this is its story, and unavoidably that of the aces themselves.

Mike Spick
July 1988

THE
ACE FACTOR

Chapter 1

The Nature of Air Combat

"The analyst and the historian share certain reservations about the accuracy of historical data. First, history is made by people, and people do not like to record their own failures, so historical data can be badly skewed by efforts to conceal human foibles. Next, warfare is a drama played without a script, concealed behind a screen of secrecy and deception, and accompanied by loud and deliberate lies and alarms. Further, the actors in the drama are far more concerned with playing their roles than recording events. Where are the truths? During any climactic episode, the various participants see different or even conflicting versions of events. Which are the truths? Finally, before one can count and mathematically manipulate large numbers of objects and events, it is necessary to define both discrete distinctions and like categories. When definitions are not carefully drawn and explicitly stated, we must be cautious in demonstrating relationships—lest we compare cabbages and kings."

Saber Measures (Charlie) (U) . . . USAF September 1970.

The most controversial subject in the entire history of air warfare is that of fighter kills. Overclaiming is a feature of all periods and all nations. There are many reasons for this, the main one being the heat and confusion of battle. There is one well-documented case of a German bomber in 1940 being attacked by no less than seven British fighters from different units in very quick succession. It crashed, and 4½ kills were awarded for this single aircraft. On the other hand, there are

1

many cases of aircraft reaching base so badly damaged that they never flew again. These were obviously "kills," but were they claimed? One thing seems to be certain; overclaiming appears to increase in proportion to the number of aircraft in the action; the higher the number of participants, the greater the level of confusion. With the benefit of hindsight, and much painstaking research, we find that in general, the claims of the high scorers are fairly accurate, while erroneous claims stem mainly from inexperienced pilots. It is reasonable to suppose that this reflects the SA or lack of it, of both parties, the aces being better able to keep track of events in a confused situation. It is equally reasonable to say that spurious claims constitute a very small proportion of the whole, and that most claims are made in good faith. The emotive word "kill" is rather at fault here; "victory" is far more acceptable and very likely a good bit more accurate. But however errors occur we just have to live with them. If we refer to "victories," we shall be more honest than if we refer to "kills," which is a much more hard and fast expression. There is little point in taking the matter further; some analysts have produced figures based on known overclaiming which may or may not be relevant. All this does is to produce figures that are purely theoretical which have been based on anticipated inaccuracies. This only serves to muddy the water still further, and has no practical application. We can only take the figures we have got as being in good faith, as aerial victories rather than the destruction of an opponent.

Air combat is far more fluid and fast-moving than any other form of warfare, and in this sense is more complex. The fact that it operates in three dimensions rather than two only serves to increase its complexity. It is all too easy for participants to gain an impression of events which is not borne out by subsequent reconstruction, hence the importance of thorough debriefing after the action. This is the "fog of war" described by Carl von Clausewitz in his monumental work *Vom Krieg*. Although Clausewitz only experienced the slow moving land warfare of the Napoleonic era, parts of his writings are very relevant to the fast, three-dimensional air battle, especially those passages dealing with what he termed "frictions in war." War is in theory a fairly precise art; unit strengths and capabilities, both friendly and hostile, are either known or can be predicted with reasonable accuracy, and probable outcomes deduced. But as Clausewitz himself wrote, "while everything about the conduct of war appears very simple in theory, in actual practice...difficulties accumulate, and end by producing a kind of friction that is inconceivable unless one has experienced war."

Clausewitz lists four main types of "friction." The first is the less than perfect intelligence, ie, situational awareness, upon which critical combat decisions must be based, which is the "fog of war." Secondly is the psychological pressures on the participants, caused by the possibility of imminent extinction. Thirdly, the physical stress of combat tends to lower efficiency. Fourthly is the demoralizing effect of the unexpected.

Translated to the specific scenario of the air battle, the first "friction" reflects a lack of SA to a greater or lesser degree, although this does tend to be a double-sided coin. In a multi-bogey situation, say more than a dozen or so participants, the confusion factor is such that it is impossible for anyone to keep track of everything that is going on around them. Some manage better than others, and the favored few far more than most. Even in a small engagement, say two versus two, it is almost impossible to be certain that other bandits will not join in, literally out of the blue. Other factors enter the equation; what is the capability of the enemy aircraft vis-a-vis one's own? In modern times, what are the relative energy states? Is the foe an ace or turkey? What are the relative fuel states? All these things add to the "fog of war."

The second "friction" is caused by man's in-built instinct for survival, and is a much neglected area of study. A fighter pilot usually "buys it" in one of two ways; in flames or in pieces, and either way it is pretty grisly. He wants to help win the war, but he also wants to be there to see it won. The survival instinct is very strong, and has often been counter-productive. There are many recorded cases of pilots taking the quick way out of the battle, and giving their adversary an easy shot in doing so. There are other instances of individuals end-ing in a disadvantageous situation through being over-cautious at a time when daring and controlled aggression would not only have had a better chance of success, but would have been the safer course.

The third "friction" is either physical tiredness, or combat fatigue. Too many sorties without rest; fighting at high altitudes without oxygen, which was the lot of the First World War scout pilots; an extended sortie over enemy territory; a protracted fight pulling high g; all these factors tend to lower the efficiency of the individual, and reduce his performance. In the case of formation leaders it is far more serious as it adversely affects the fighting efficiency of the entire unit, and can also lower morale.

The fourth "friction" is in many ways the most important; the demoralizing effect of the unexpected. The combatant thinks that he has the situation under control when he suddenly realizes that all is not as it seems. The classic case is of a fighter pilot diving on an unsuspecting opponent, taking careful aim, then hearing bullets tearing through this craft from behind. The tables are instantly turned! From a good attacking position he finds himself in a poor defensive position in the twinkling of an eye. This sort of shock action is effective in all forms of warfare, and in extreme cases it has been known to paralyze the thought processes of the victim, making him incapable of further resistance. Shock action, or surprise, is in fact the dominant factor in air combat, and we will return to this later. Its effect cannot possibly be overrated.

The overall effect of all these "frictions" is to lower the theoretical performance of the combatants by an unquantifiable amount, interrupting the smooth running of the war machine. Fighting in the air is to a great degree a matter of teamwork, and just one member of the team performing below his best will jeopardize the entire formation. SA is the factor which minimizes "frictions" dispelling if not entirely dissipating the "fog of war," helping the pilot to instinctively do the right thing under stress, partially offsetting the effects of fatigue, and anticipating and avoiding the unexpected. If a formation leader has a high level of SA, this will spread itself across the entire group, raising their effectiveness by a considerable margin.

Leaders and leadership are subjects which crop up continually in air fighting. Obviously quality varies greatly, but at the highest level a top leader can have an effect out of all proportion on his unit, which he will weld into a cohesive fighting unit with a sum much greater than the total of its individual parts. His main contribution, apart from ordering the tactics to be used, is to improve morale and thus minimize the effects of "frictions." Even if he is unable to dispel the fog of war, or guard against the effects of shock action, a good leader will hearten his men and rally them in an unfavorable situation.

In its early days, air fighting was often likened to a sport. This is a very misleading analogy. Sport has two distinct connotations. The first is a contest held in a finite arena, to carefully defined rules, between individuals or numerically even teams, equally well equipped, with the result decided either by superior strength or skill. Air combat is nothing like this. The arena is limited only by the performance of the aircraft involved, and one may be far better than the other. There is no umpire to see fair play; there is no fair play! There is only one rule which says "if you can't win, survive." As a contestant enters the arena, he must expect to be jumped on from the top of the grandstand without warning, and if he sees that the opposing team have enlisted King Kong, it is quite permissible to return instantly to the dressing room and come back on the morrow when circumstances might be more favorable. As US Navy ace Randy Cunningham is fond of saying, "there are no prizes for second place."

The other meaning of sport is a little nearer; that of hunting, shooting and fishing, but not a lot. In these activities, risk to the participants is minimal, which is far from the case in air warfare. The successful air fighter does his best to load the scales in his own favor, but can never be completely certain of the outcome, as even the slightest error can make him the prey rather than the hunter. It is very noticeable that the First World War aces who talk most about sport are the ones who get most upset if an opponent breaks what they see as the rules; for example the Red Baron when the observer of a force-landed British aircraft fired back at him from the ground, or Canadian

Billy Bishop when German observation machines tried to sucker him into an ambush. By contrast, James McCudden observed that he was forced to subordinate his sporting instincts in favor of efficient killing, which after all, is what war is about.

Another myth prevalent at this time was that of the Chivalry of the Air. Compared to the amorphous mass carnage on the ground, the air war was comparatively clean and personal. Fighter pilots of all nations tend to have one thing in common; a love of flying. To this extent they form a brotherhood of the air, but in times of war, this does not prevent them from acts of desperate fratricide. In the early days of the First World War, they sometimes waved to each other at a point in the combat where both were jockeying for position, while the entertaining of captured enemy pilots was fairly commonplace. This did not prevent them from doing their level best to sneak up on each other unobserved and shoot each other in the back when opportunity offered. There is no sportsmanship, and no chivalry in this; it is the method of the assassin rather than the knight, but it is demanded by combat efficiency; the need to do as much damage as possible at as little risk. A considerable number of high-scoring First World War aces felt badly about this, and tended to play up the chivalric and sporting image as a result, probably as a form of mental self-protection. Many

The notion of chivalry in the air bore about as much relationship to air combat as this cartoon, although courtesy could be, and often was, extended to a vanquished foe once he was safely on the ground.

were revolted when an opponent went down in flames, especially when ambushed and shot down without any chance of hitting back. Guilt was combined with the ever-present thought that one day it might well be their turn. The chivalric myth was further perpetuated by memoirs and biographies, which tended to dwell on the more difficult, maneuvering combats at the expense of the more common swift and deadly strikes against a foe taken unawares. There are plenty of reasons for this. The maneuver combats, or dogfights as they are generally known, tend to be more interesting and make better reading, whereas the first pass victories get progressively more dull and repetitious as they continue to occur.

There was in fact slightly more room for chivalry in the Second World War, when pilots were uniformly equipped with parachutes. It was generally considered bad form to shoot at a defeated pilot descending to earth beneath his brolly, in spite of the fact that he was over his own territory and might be back in action on the following day. There was absolutely no excuse for trying to kill a pilot descending over hostile territory, as he could be captured, and had become effectively a non-combatant, but the exigencies of war demanded that one who might be back in action very quickly, be dealt with. On the other hand, there may have been an element of self-preservation in the non-observance of this harsh necessity; one never knew when the roles might be reversed. The killing of an unarmed and defenseless pilot on the end of a parachute was usually looked upon with revulsion; this type of total war is foreign to the nature of civilized men, and while war brutalizes, the type of man who flies fighters is too much of an individualist to be totally affected. There were always exceptions. The Samurai code of Bushido stated that a warrior who allowed himself to be captured had lost all honor, and that a pilot who abandoned his crippled aircraft was somehow less than a man, and had forfeited all honor. He was therefore fair game. On the Russian front, the air war was fought with much hatred, and finer feelings were not much in evidence. In more modern times, as aircraft have got faster and their weaponry more deadly and complicated, the idea of chivalry has long been abandoned. The fighter pilot of today is a highly trained

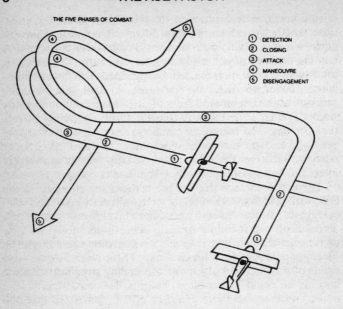

THE FIVE PHASES OF COMBAT

① DETECTION
② CLOSING
③ ATTACK
④ MANEOUVRE
⑤ DISENGAGEMENT

The five phases of air combat. (1) Detection. (2) Closing. (3) Attack. (4) Maneuver. (5) Disengagement.

technician who controls a weapons system rather than an airplane. There is no time for empty gestures.

Air combat is usually broken down into five distinct but not immutable phases. These are: a) Detection; b) Closing; c) Attack; d) Maneuver; and e) Disengagement. The sequence varies according to the individual circumstance; for example, detecting an enemy who has reached the attack phase would instantly be followed by maneuver, while if he had merely reached a favorable position in his closing phase, the best option might be disengagement.

Detection is the first phase, and in many ways is the most important of all. Detecting the enemy before being detected by him gives the initiative, which in turn allows the fighter pilot to try and attain the advantage of surprise. On detecting a hostile machine or formation, the pilot must assess the situation; whether it is favorable for attack or not. Many factors enter into this; relative numerical strengths, relative attitudes, and the chances of achieving a successful surprise bounce. Is the situation what it seems, or is that solitary machine ambling around down sun at a lower altitude, the bait in a well prepared ambush, with a dozen of his mates standing guard higher up? Or is he the Red Baron himself, supremely confident in his own abilities, trying to lure an inexperienced young flyer into a close combat to which there will be but one outcome? This is what SA is all about, and the penalty for guessing wrongly is high, although the rewards for guessing rightly are correspondingly great. Having detected, the decision must be made whether or not to attack. Or course, circumstances will always arise where the needs of the mission dictate that an attack must be made, whether the circumstances are favorable or not, and in this case the only course of action is to load the dice as far as is practicable, even if this is not much. The small print on a fighter pilot's graduation certificate does not include a guarantee of longevity.

In World War 1, the only means of detection was visual. The aircraft were small, and even in condition of perfect visibility were difficult to see at more than two miles' range, although a formation could be seen at double this distance. Haze could on occasion reduce this distance to half a mile or so. The eye tends to pick out relative movement more easily than a stationary object, particularly in the peripheral vision. An aircraft approaching from exactly head-on, or going away tail-on, would therefore be more difficult to acquire than one moving at an angle. An aircraft flying directly at its intended victim would not only be more difficult to see, but would also constitute by far the greater threat.

It did, of course, help if the pilot knew in which direction to look, although too much concentration in one direction was dangerous. The bursts of anti-aircraft shellfire were often used as indicators of enemy activity, and these could lead a fighter pilot towards his prey. In the Second World War, radar coupled with ground control was of the greatest assistance in making contact, while since that time, airborne early warning

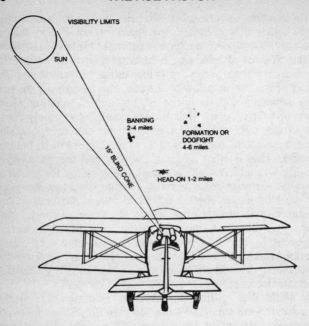

This gives some idea of visibility limits for First World War aircraft. A single aircraft from head or tail-on could be picked out at between one and two miles. If banking this distance would double, a formation or a dogfight would often be visible from between four and six miles. The sun always caused a blind cone about fifteen degrees wide. The human eyeball has not changed, and these limits still apply for comparable sized aircraft.

combined with on-board radar has enabled fighters to make contact with their opponents at up to a hundred miles, and attacks to be made from well beyond visual distance. The one thing that has not changed is that he who sees first, by whatever means, has greater SA, which in turn gives him the initiative.

Having made the decision to attack, the next phase of combat consists of closing the distance to a point from which an attack can be made. In fact, it is rather difficult to tell where the closing phase ends and the attack phase begins, as they tend to merge imperceptibly into each other. It would probably be true to say that the closing phase lasts for the time in which it is possible to reverse the decision to attack, which may be made for any number of reasons; a drop in oil pressure, the sudden appearance of further hostile forces or whatever. The whole essence of closing is to avoid discovery in order to maintain the disparity in SA between the attacker and the attacked, or put more simply, to achieve surprise.

There are many ways in which this can be done. Approaching the victim from the rear may help, especially from below, where his vision is shielded by his own aircraft. The sun has been used from time immemorial; it is very difficult to see an aircraft which is flying within a fifteen degree cone centered on the sun. Cloud can also be useful stuff, but it means that sight of the target must be lost for a greater or lesser period, during which he might change course and be lost forever. In modern times, it often means lurking "down in the weeds" away from the prying eyes of enemy radars, and it certainly means staying out of the search area of the intended victim's radar. ECM is all very well, but it is an emission, and may easily give the game away. Nor is shining one's own radar on him for protracted periods a good idea, as he will soon know that someone is looking at him with hostile intent, and from which direction. The radar on standby, with occasional sweeps to keep track of what is going on, is quite enough. If no means of using stealth are available, the only course is to close as quickly as possible, reducing the time available for the victim to see the attacker coming.

The third phase of air combat is attack, and this is often decisive. The historical record shows that four out of every five pilots shot down never saw their attacker until too late, if at all. This is of course basically fighter versus fighter combat, or fighter versus reconnaissance aircraft or artillery spotter. It would be very difficult, if not impossible, to surprise bombers flying in formation; they have too many eyes searching the sky in all directions, but on the other hand, they are not free to maneuver against an attack. That about eighty per-

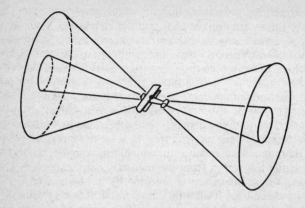

The best gun attack angles in any war have been from astern or ahead, within fifteen degree cone of the target centerline for preference, while within a 45 degree cone was better than nothing. Outside this, few could hit anything. Examination of the literature of air combat shows that the aces took a lot more head-on shots than is popularly supposed.

cent of all victims fall at this stage is very impressive, and graphically illustrates the value of surprise and shock action. It is also the end product of early detection and concealed closing.

The method of attack is dictated by the nature of the weapons carried. For the first four decades, the main fighter weapon was the fixed forward-firing gun, at first small caliber weapons mounted singly or in pairs, later supplanted by batteries of six or eight machine-guns, and finally by lesser numbers of larger caliber weapons of 20 mm and upwards. Very few people ever mastered the art of deflection shooting with any degree of reliability, and the most usual method of obtaining results was to get in close astern of the target for a no-deflection shot. This was also preferable against a single seater which had no rearward-firing guns.

From about 1955, the homing missile gradually started taking over from the gun as the main fighter weapon. Guidance systems for these were of two main types; semi-active radar homing, which was effective from medium ranges, preferably from head-on, and which could be used from beyond visual range; and the shorter-ranged infra-red homer which was best fired from astern. Many aircraft were designed with no gun, as the test results obtained with the new missiles were so impressive that there seemed little need for such a close range, limited capability weapon; but after some unfortunate experiences in actual combat, the gun was quickly reinstated as an essential part of the fighter's armory. At first the homing missiles were only effective against non-maneuvering targets, but this has been greatly improved over the past fifteen years or so. The latest missiles are advertised as being "all-aspect," although they still have limitations. An essential part of situational awareness is for the pilot to know exactly what his weapons are capable of in varying circumstances against different targets; and even more important, what he, personally, can do with them.

Fourth in the list of combat phases comes maneuver. This is the realm of the dogfight, the exciting and spectacular close combat arena, where according to popular legend the aces reign supreme, sending victim after victim down in a welter of fire and dismembered wings. Rather less excitingly, it is also the phase in which less than twenty percent of victories are scored.

Maneuver combat occurs in three circumstances; firstly when neither side gains a decisive advantage in early detection; secondly when concealment during the closing phase fails; and thirdly when the attacker makes a hash of his attack. The nature of the dogfight varies both with the numbers involved, and the period in which it takes place. Stated simply, it involves trying to outmaneuver an opponent in order to gain a good shooting position, which traditionally has meant onto his tail. Turning ability is above all a function of speed; the slower the speed, the tighter the turn. There are, however, limits, the most important of which is the minimum flying speed, at which the aircraft can do no more that waffle along straight and level, with no maneuver capability at all. Hard turning creates drag, which tends to slow the aircraft. This is a process that cannot be allowed to continue, as the fighter will inevitably reach minimum flying speed sooner or later, and will be left with no capability at all, either offensive or defensive. It will become a sitting duck. One alternative is to trade altitude for speed, although this cannot be continued indefinitely, as sooner or later the ground will intervene. The well-trained pilot has a whole bag of tricks to enable him to avoid being trapped by a better turning opponent. These are currently known as basic fighter maneuvers, which have been developed and refined over many years.

Over the years, the volume of sky in which a dogfight takes place has increased out of all recognition, due to increased aircraft speeds and higher wing loadings. The typical First World War dogfight took place in a cylinder of sky about half a mile across, into which fifty or sixty fighters might be packed. Mid-air collisions were a fairly frequent occurrence, and pilots spent an undue proportion of their time avoiding them. A law of diminishing returns seemed to operate; the number of casualities expressed as a percentage of the total number of aircraft involved was in inverse proportion to the total number of participants. A two versus two encounter might easily end with one airplane shot down, whereas a twenty-five versus thirty might see only three or four losses, even though these big engagements often lasted for twenty minutes or more. The reason for this is not hard to find. In a small numbers encounter it was not too hard to keep track of what was going on, whereas with a sky full of angrily diving and turning fighters, it was simply impossible. In, say, a four versus five, it was possible to latch onto one opponent and try to out-maneuver him for as much as half a minute, or even more, before being forced to break off. In the big battle, more than two or three seconds was enough to give an adversary time to slip in behind and open fire. This, coupled with the need to avoid collisions with friend as well as foe, gave little time for anything other than a snap-shot at a crossing target as opportunity offered. One man simply could not keep track of events, regardless of how gifted he might be. In a nutshell, SA could be maintained in limited numbers fights, but dropped to nil in a multi-bogey situation. Most of the pilot's attention in the big affairs was concentrated on survival rather than notching up a score. It is noticeable that most of the very high scoring aces tried to keep out of the confused, whirling fight, and contented themselves with trying to pick off stragglers. This is also a form of SA; the aces were very aware of their own limitations, and tended to keep out of situations with which they could not cope adequately.

Dogfights in the Second World War had many of the same ingredients as those of the first, especially as far as confusion was concerned, but they were generally much briefer and occupied a volume of sky three or four times larger in diameter, and half as high again. Generally the numbers involved were rather smaller, and the rates of turn were slower, due to the higher fighting speeds. The weapons were longer ranged and more deadly, and this partly compensated for what was arguably a slower paced fight. Teamwork came into its own far more than formerly, aided immeasurably by air-to-air radio communications. A section leader was far more able to concentrate on scoring knowing that his wingman was looking after his tail and could radio a warning if trouble loomed. It was during this conflict that night fighting first became a practical proposition, thanks to the development of radar. While radar was not an all-seeing eye, able to turn night into day, it was able to give situational awareness under circumstances where none had previously existed.

The next dogfights of any note took place in the stratosphere over North Korea. Speeds had increased still more, while turn rates had dropped dramatically in the thin air. Weaponry had not kept pace with the advances in speed and altitude, and pilots found it remarkably difficult to get into a good shooting position. Large formations were found to be impossible to manage successfully, and attempts were made to saturate the contested area with pairs or fours. The dogfight in most cases became a succession of brief skirmishes with successive elements, spread over an enormous area of the sky, although there were occasional protracted encounters between individuals or pairs.

It was thought by many that the advent of homing missiles, able to follow their targets as they maneuvered, would end the dogfight. Experience in many limited wars around the world

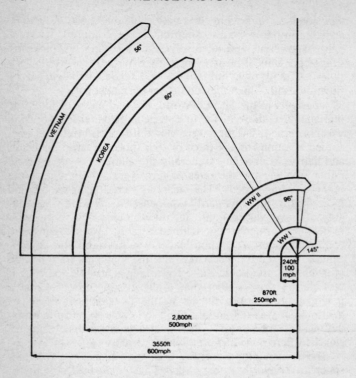

As combat speeds increased, turn capabilities diminished and the pace of maneuver combat actually reduced. Shown here to scale are typical turn radii, with the angle-off produced in four seconds, of four conflicts; World Wars 1 and 2, Korea and Vietnam. Although much lip service has always been paid to the importance of maneuver, until recent times it took second place to performance.

soon exposed the falsity of this, and close combat is still a viable proposition today, although it must be admitted that it would hardly be recognized as a dogfight by a veteran of 1917. The fighter pilot is becoming more and more reliant on clever electronics, force multipliers such as AWACS, and other gadgetry, to let him know what is going on around him, and his SA lies mainly in the ability to make use of the presented information.

Disengagement is the final phase of air combat, and is where the remaining victories are scored. This phase has traditionally been the least considered of all, yet it is one of the most important, in survival terms if nothing else. In the days of the gun-armed fighter, it was either stuffing down the nose and accelerating away out of range, or picking one's moment to make a break for it. Judging the moment was the difficult part; it had to be a time when the fight was drifting in the opposite direction to the way one wanted to go, in order to open up an instant gap. Many pilots have been lost simply because they chose the wrong direction, even though the other circumstances were favorable. Flying deeper into enemy territory instead of away from it was generally not very helpful unless one's aircraft was either considerably faster, or had a much better climb rate than those of the opposition.

In the faster monoplane fighters of the Second World War, disengagement was often inadvertent. The greatly increased speeds served to take a fighter that turned in the opposite direction to the general drift of the engagement, out of the fight with a rapidity that was quite bewildering; one moment a sky full of aircraft; the next, empty. Even in this war, disengagement was never given the attention that it deserved.

The missile age changed attitudes out of all recognition. An ill-considered plunge from the squirrel cage could very easily be rewarded by a heat-seeking missile in the flue, and the long reach of these new weapons made it difficult, if not impossible, to simply accelerate away out of range. Very fine judgement was called for. At the same time, the colossal fuel consumption of the new breed of fighter made disengagement far more important than at any time in the past. The modern fighter driver has to attempt to make his opponent lose sight of him, thereby destroying his SA, before attempting to disengage. In practice this is not as bad as it seems, as the high speeds and large turn radii of the aircraft in the dogfight mean that they are often operating at the extreme limits of visibility. Radar is still a factor, but there are many ways of defeating this. The clever bit is in knowing whether the method adopted has worked!

We have examined air combat from an individual angle; the viewpoint of the flyer. We should equally examine it as a whole, from the command point of view. Air force commanders have to wield their weapons to the best effect, just as the man in the front line has to, but the fact that their weapons are whole air forces rather complicates the situation. The commanders have to deal with individuals *en masse,* and are forced to concern themselves with units rather than persons. In war, losses are inevitable, and some must be accepted. It is the commander's responsibility to carry out his allotted tasks with the forces available for the minimum losses. One of the most intractable problems concerns force ratios.

It is a matter of simple logic to suggest that in a bar-room brawl, two men will beat one man, almost every time. Yet when one tries to apply this principle to warfare, and examines the historical record, it very often comes unglued. All else being equal, the big battalions should win every time, the degree of certainty bearing a direct relationship to the amount by which the smaller force is outnumbered, but in practice, the outcome seems far less predictable. On the other hand, it should be noted that this applies more to battles than to wars. Wars won by a nation which is numerically weaker than its opponent tend to be finished quickly, in circumstances where either single encounter, or a short series of battles destroys either the capability or the will of the enemy to resist. Where resistance is continued, the war degenerates into a process of attrition in which the big battalions have the advantage.

Down the years many people, often with practical experience, have tried to reduce the conduct of battles to the level of chess, where a certain move elicits a predictable response. This century has been no exception; the leading theoretician at the birth of war in the air being F.W. Lanchester, whose influence on the conduct of air fighting lasted into the Second World War. Lanchester, an engineer and mathematician, postulated theories based on the "concentration of firepower" effect, which is directly related to force ratios. These are still used today for wargames and simulations, for want of anything better, and given parity in pilot quality, leadership, equipment, and tactics, would probably be fairly valid for predicting outcomes in the real thing. What are these theories, and how do they work?

The original formula postulated by Lanchester is embodied in a pair of differential equations designed to calculate the attrition rate for both sides during a battle. There were in fact three different hypotheses. The first is known as the linear law, which states that the attrition rate in terms of losses per hour or day throughout an engagement is constant. The second is the logarithmic law, which states that the attrition rate is a constant percentage of the surviving forces of one side, irrespective of the opposing strength. The third, and most widely used, is the n^2 law, which states that the attrition rate is constant but multiplied by the surviving strength of the adversary.

The first thing that we notice about all three hypotheses is that they are all heavily dependent upon attrition, and factors such as weapons characteristics, fire-power and training are largely ignored. The linear law can be immediately discounted as it assumes that losses are independent of the size of the force sustaining them, and takes no account of the quality versus quantity debate, of which more later. Nor is the logarithmic law much better as the opposing force strength is ignored. The n^2 law works better in theory, which is why it has survived as a modelling tool for so long, but how does it stand up against the test of actual combat?

A cursory skim through the records and literature of air combat will give literally hundreds of instances where the few beat the many; for example, three fighters attacking five and shooting down two without loss. In most cases, the dual factors of surprise and shock action can be seen to be decisive, but not always. On the other hand, a short encounter in the air is not a war; it is hardly a campaign, and often constitutes only a small part of a battle. Are there any records which would prove or disprove the n^2 law? Do they even prove the value of force ratios? The following table has been abstracted from the USAF study Saber Measures (Charlie), and relates to selected campaigns of the Second World War. It covers air to air sorties only, with victory and loss rates.

Force ratios are given based on the Allied sortie rate, while

Campaign	Total sorties		Force ratio	Victory ratio		Loss ratio	
	Allies	Axis		Allies	Axis	Allies	Axis
France 1940 10 May/20 June	4,480	21,000	1:4.69	2.86	1.25	5.85	0.61
Battle of Britain 10 July/31 Oct	31,000	42,000	1:1.35	2.66	2.18	2.95	1.96
AVG China/Burma Dec 41/July 42	6,000	2,000	3:1	2.13	0.60	0.20	6.40
NW Australia Feb 42/March 43	300	400	1:1.33	2.00	4.74	6.33	1.50
Coral Sea May 1942	227	160	1.42:1	5.73	13.13	9.25	8.13
Midway, June 1942	90	120	1:1.33	8.89	5.00	6.67	6.67
New Guinea Feb/Aug 1942	1,900	1,000	1.9:1	2.16	17.70	9.32	4.10
Guadalcanal Aug 42/Feb 43	1,759	1,869	1:1.06	7.73	4.23	4.49	7.28
New Britain Sep 42/June 43	8,600	4,000	2.15:1	4.42	2.85	1.33	9.50
Rabaul Oct 43/Feb 44	5,345	2,400	2.23:1	6.17	4.67	2.10	13.75
Western Europe 6 April/5 June 44	98,400	34,500	2.85:1	1.27	2.93	1.03	3.61
Western Europe 6 June/5 Sep 44	203,357	31,833	6.39:1	1.73	1.62	0.25	11.06

victory and loss ratios are given in aircraft per 100 sorties. It should be noted that the actual numbers of aircraft taking part are not used. It is of little point to outnumber the enemy on the ground as this only provides targets; the object of the exercise is to outnumber him in the air, which is where it really counts. The number of sorties is a far more accurate measure of strength, as it accounts for the factors of more maintainable aircraft, better logistics, etc. It is also a fact that up to the present day, air forces tend to get run out of pilots rather than aircraft, which also makes sorties far more relevant than the inventory of available hardware, although in future conflicts this may not be the case. The complexity of modern fighters compared to that of their forebears means that construction time will be considerably longer, and the factories may no longer be able to keep pace with the anticipated rate of attrition.

The tabular data should be treated with a certain amount of caution before conclusions can be drawn. Firstly, although it relates only to fighter sorties, in some cases the losses include those that fell to the guns of bombers. This is almost certainly so for the Battle of Britain figures and also those for the post D-Day Western Europe campaign. In other cases, certainly for Midway, the losses are from fighter versus fighter encounters. Secondly, a large proportion of the campaigns are lopsided in that one side was almost entirely defensive while the other was attacking. In these instances, the priority for the defending fighters would be the enemy bombers, with the escorting fighters regarded as secondary, and held off as best they could be. Bearing these two points in mind, we can see if any pattern emerges.

Just two campaigns out of the twelve show a decisive force disparity. France during the seven weeks following the start of the Blitzkrieg in 1940, in which the Luftwaffe enjoyed a superior force ratio of just under 5:1, and Western Europe during the three months following D-Day. It should of course be understood that the figures do not include the night battle over the Reich. In the summer of 1944, the Allies had a superior force ratio of more than 6:1.

While it cannot be denied that the big battalions were on the winning side in both cases, application of any of the Lanchestrian laws would show virtual annihilation of the weaker forces in short order. This was patently not the case. The Battle of France was lost because the ground forces were over-run, while after the invasion of Europe, the German fighter force took a terrible hammering it is true, but it remained in being as a formidable, if weakened, adversary. This poses the question; why in each case were not the weaker forces swept from the skies in a matter of days?

The answer can be sought in the comparative victory and loss ratios. During the Blitzkrieg in France, the out-numbered Allied fighters achieved a victory ratio per 100 sorties of more than double that of the Luftwaffe. In the later campaign, the even more heavily outnumbered Luftwaffe almost attained parity, and if we were to take into account the bombers shot down by them, this figure would be far more favorable. The reason for this apparent anomaly lies in the number of opportunities available; the outnumbered force had far more chances; they operated in a "target rich" environment. The loss figures per 100 sorties tell a much sadder story; they were ten times and 44 times worse respectively, than those of their opponents. The actual loss figures give a truer story. A total of 262 Allied and 128 German fighters were lost in air combat in France between the Blitzkrieg opening and the start of the air battles over Dunkirk; a ratio of 2.05:1 which, when one considers the force disadvantage, reflects very creditably on the Allies. For the post-D-Day period, the figures were 516 Allied losses to 3,521 German, which is in proportion to the sortie ratio.

Are there any other factors which could have affected the issue? It is certainly true that many fighter pilots who flew with the larger forces got little or no chance to score. Oberleutnant Julius Neumann, who flew Me 109s in 1940, later commented "We saw very few enemy fighters during this period and those we did see were not handled very aggressively." This is, of course, a subjective judgement, and may well mean that the fighters encountered had no intention of letting themselves be trapped at a numerical or tactical disadvantage. By contrast, the Western Europe campaign in 1944 was far more intense, the average daily number of sorties being flown was more than four times as many, over a rather smaller area for the most part. It was therefore far more difficult for the heavily outnumbered Luftwaffe fighter pilots to avoid combat if the situation was unfavorable. The main difference between these two campaigns, however, which took place during the first and the last full years of the war, was undoubtedly of pilot quality. The Blitzkrieg campaign in 1940 was fought out between high quality, peacetime-trained and very experienced pilots on both sides. In this the Luftwaffe had the edge, as many of their pilots had had combat experience in either Spain or Poland, where many tactical lessons had also been learned. By the summer of 1944, with the exception of a handful of experienced and battle-hardened leaders on both sides, the majority of fighter pilots had received a rather sketchy, wartime training, and were inexperienced. In this respect the Luftwaffe was by far the worst off, with their training schedule disrupted by fuel shortages. It is said of this period that the Luftwaffe had only two sorts of fighter pilots; the hard core of *experten*, highly experienced and very dangerous opponents, and the novices, who were little more than cannon fodder.

Moving down the force ratio scale we have two campaigns lying around the 3:1 mark; that of the American Volunteer Group flying against the Japanese over China and Burma between December 1, 1941 and July 5, 1942; and the battle for air superiority over western Europe prior to D-Day, lasting from April 6 until June 5, 1944. There the resemblance ends; the Far Eastern campaign consisted of some 8,000 sorties in total spread over 218 days, an average of 37 sorties per day, while in Europe 132,900 sorties were packed into just sixty days, giving an intensity almost sixty times greater.

The Flying Tigers, as the AVG was known, had what was convincingly the best of things, scoring 128 victories for twelve losses, with a victory per hundred sorties rate of 2.13 which, although not spectacular by the standards of the times, was nearly four times better than their Japanese opponents achieved, while their loss ratio was no less than 32 *times* better. In Western Europe prior to D-Day, it was a completely different story. Despite the numerical difference, the total losses were very closely matched; the Allied Air Forces losing 1,102 fighters and the Luftwaffe 1,246. This can be regarded as a points victory for the Luftwaffe, as a considerable number of their pilots survived to fight again, while almost all those of the Allies who baled out or force-landed successfully were marched off to a POW camp for the duration. In terms of victory ratios and loss ratios, the German pilots emerged with credit, with more than twice as many victories per 100 sorties, although losing in terms of fighter aircraft some 3½ times as many as the Allies. With fighters pouring off the production lines this was not too serious. While the loss of experienced pilots was bad, and was in the end to prove unsupportable, taking this campaign in isolation, if it was to be judged by the number of pilots lost to either side, it would seem to be a German victory. Yet when one considers the broad picture, it was the beginning of the end. From D-Day onwards, the Allies stepped up their fighter effort by about fifty percent, whereas the German effort fell by roughly the same amount, with the effect that the force ratio against the German flyers more than doubled, with the results that we have seen.

Coming still further down the scale of force ratios, there are three campaigns which have sortie ratios of around 2:1, all of which took place in the Pacific theater, and all show an Allied force superiority. In chronological order they are: Eastern New Guinea between February 1 and August 31, 1942, a period of around thirty weeks; New Britain and New Guinea from September 15, 1942 to June 30, 1943, a protracted 41-week struggle following on from the earlier campaign; and Rabaul, lasting from October 1, 1943 to February 17, 1944, a total of twenty weeks. These three run on from each other fairly closely, and from a desultory start in Eastern New Guinea with an average sortie rate of fourteen per day including both sides, the tempo steps up to 44 sorties per day for New Britain and 55 per day for Rabaul. This is a far cry from the air battles over Western Europe, and so are the results.

From the Allied point of view, New Guinea started more as a holding action which gradually switched over to the offensive. The Japanese had both the best fighters and the most experienced pilots, and this was reflected in the losses, 177 Allied to only 41 Japanese. The Japanese victories per 100 sorties ratio was extremely high, at nearly eighteen, more than eight times better than that of the Allied forces. At the same time, their loss ratio per 100 sorties was high at over four, although that of the Allies was more than double. From this we can deduce that the Japanese pilots concentrated on attack at the expense of defense, although a victory figure of four enemy aircraft shot down for each friendly lost would appear to justify this approach, especially when faced with an adverse sortie ratio of nearly 2:1.

The New Britain campaign saw the Allies switch very definitely to the offensive. Force was met with force, and while the sortie ratio swung even further in favor of the Allies, the increase was marginal. Respective losses were 114 Allied and

380 Japanese; the wheel had swung full circle. Victories per 100 sorties rose to nearly 4½ for the Allies, dropping dramatically to under three for the Japanese, while the Japanese losses per 100 sorties more than doubled but those of the Allies fell by a factor of seven. This reversal of fortunes can be attributed to three things: firstly, better fighters were appearing on the Allied side; secondly the leadership was better, while thirdly, the increased tempo of operations, the bigger and messier multi-bogey dogfights did not suit the Japanese style nor their equipment.

Finally we have Rabaul, with a yet faster tempo of air fighting, and the fortunes of war going ever further the Allies' way. The Allies lost a total of 112 fighters; the Japanese 330. That the Rabaul campaign was hard-fought we can have no doubt. The Allied victory ratio per 100 sorties increased by nearly fifth percent over that achieved in New Britain, but that of the Japanese improved even more. Loss ratios also increased from those of the earlier conflict; the Allies by nearly sixty percent and the Japanese by a massive seventy percent, to an unprecedented 13.75 losses per 100 sorties.

The final batch of campaigns yet to be examined are those in which the sortie ratios are nearly even; those less than 1.5:1. The first of these is the Battle of Britain, taken somewhat arbitrarily as lasting from July 10, 1940 to the following October 30. In terms of sorties, the Luftwaffe held a slight numerical edge over the Royal Air Force. Fighter losses on each side were 915 British and 823 German, but this is far from the whole picture. The British fighters had radar and ground-controlled interception to help them, while the German fighters generally had both position and altitude, which is generally considered to be the decisive factor in air combat, although they were short on range and were unable to hang about long once the fight had started. Finally, and most important, the primary targets of the German fighters were the British fighters, whereas the primary targets of the British fighters were the German bombers. It is therefore fair to say that the odds were stacked against the Royal Air Force, insofar as fighter combat went. In terms of victories and losses per 100 sorties, the results are unimpressive in cold figures, the respective victory ratios being 2.66 for the British and 2.18 for the Germans, while the loss ratios were 2.95 and 1.96 respectively. Perspective is only gained when it is considered that the total Luftwaffe losses of all types in air combat total around 1,600 for this period, and that in spite of the best efforts of the German fighter pilots to prevent it, bomber attrition rose to unacceptable levels. The average fighter density was very high, around 640 sorties per day including both sides, which made the fighting messy and confused for the most part. In battles of this nature, the more confused the situation, the lower both the victory and loss ratios become, as we have seen before.

Next in chronological order is the defense of Northern Australia and Darwin against the Japanese. A total of only 700 sorties was flown in just short of 400 days, and the fighting took the form of sporadic air raids which were met as required by the forces available. Fighter losses during this period were nineteen Australian and just six Japanese. Loss ratios for this campaign were 6.33 Australian and 1.50 for the Japanese.

The next two battles in this series are both fought between opposing carrier forces; Coral Sea in May 1942, and Midway the following month. In naval terms, Coral Sea was indecisive, whereas Midway, a disaster for the Japanese, can reasonably be regarded as the turning point in the Pacific War. By contrast, the fighter-versus-fighter action was a sideshow, with relatively few sorties flown by either side. The only feature of real interest is that in both cases, the outnumbered side came out on top, American losses being 21 at Coral Sea and six at Midway compared to Japanese losses of thirteen and eight respectively. Victory and loss ratios also reversed. It should however be noted that in both cases, the fighters were mainly engaged in carrying out their primary task; shooting down bombers.

Last but not least comes Guadalcanal, which is interesting if only for the fact that the number of sorties flown by each side is almost identical, the Japanese having a marginal edge of just six percent. The intensity of the fighting was low, averaging just under twenty sorties a day between the opponents, over the 186 days of the campaign. It had started at a much higher level, but quickly dropped. Losses were 79 American to 136 Japanese, giving loss ratios of 4.49 and 7.28 respectively, with marginally better victory ratios.

Do any patterns emerge from this data? At first sight, not a lot. As a generalization, the side with the greatest numerical strength tends to gain more victories than its weaker opponent, although this was certainly not the case in the early Pacific War battles. This can be directly attributed to the respective qualities of both pilots and equipment, as the trend reversed later in the war, after many of the Japanese veterans of the war in China had been lost, while the Americans gained experience and their fighters improved. What there certainly is not is a direct statistical link between force ratios, victories and losses. Nor is there any apparent connection between force ratios and rates of attrition. There is, however, a trend linked to the intensity of operations in that both victories and losses per 100 sorties decrease as the average number of sorties flown per day rises, in a sort of law of diminishing returns. But this is only a trend; not an absolute fact. This could be accounted for by the confusion factor, which is believed by many to increase in direct proportion to the square of the number of participants.

Survival of the individual is an oft overlooked factor in any consideration of air combat, and is far more important than most analysts and commentators credit. Survival is very important to the individual; he has only one life to lose, and that possibly in a most unpleasant way, whereas a victory will wait for another day. The more confused the fighting, the harder the pilot has to work to stay alive, and the less he has time available to act offensively. The opposite is also true. The smaller the engagement the less confusing it is, and the more opportunity the individual pilot has to be aggressive. As this is also true for the adversary the sky becomes a much more dangerous place for all concerned.

To summarize, superior numbers (or superior sortie rates) do not necessarily guarantee victory; the disastrous (for the Allies) New Guinea campaign of 1942 demonstrates that conclusively. The Japanese, outnumbered by almost two to one, exacted four times as many kills, with a victory per 100 sorties rate no less than *eight times* better than that of the Allies, while their loss rate per 100 sorties was less than half. Attrition rates cannot therefore be linked to numerical strength as a means of predicting the outcome of a battle or campaign. Numerical strength, or numerical superiority, matters more in an air campaign than in a single engagement, but it does not appear to be the critical factor. Nor in fact does superior equipment to any great degree, although it helps. The dominant factor in air campaigns, as in small dogfights or other engagements, lies in pilot quality.

It may be argued that the tabular data supplied, coming entirely from the Second World War, is relevant only to that conflict, and did not apply in the earlier set-to, and no longer applies today. Is any data available from both earlier or later periods which would confirm either the general trend or lack of it? The short answer to this is yes!

The air over Korea has been very well documented, and reasonably accurate figures are available from July 1951 until the end of the conflict just over two years later. There are several features of outstanding interest from the fight-versus-fighter standpoint, not the least of which is that the data is available on a month by month basis. Also the bulk of the fighting took place divorced from the ground battle, at stratospheric altitudes in a limited area adjoining the borders of North Korea and the Peoples Republic of China. It is therefore "pure" air combat between fighters to a far greater degree than any conflict before or since. Finally it was fought largely between just two fighter types; the American F-86 Sabre and the Russian MiG-15. These factors remove many of the variables that beset analysis in other periods.

The figures for the period of the war at right show the total USAF victories as 757, for losses of 103 while operating at an average force advantage of just under 2:1. The operational intensity was high, peaking at an average for the combined forces of both sides of 219 sorties a day during May 1953, and never dropping below 100 sorties a day after October 1951.

How does the Korean War data compare with that of the

		Sorties		Force	Victory ratios		Loss ratios	
		USAF	Comm	ratio	USAF	Comm	USAF	Comm
1951	July	1,011	369	2.74:1	0.79	0.27	0.10	2.17
	Aug	1,148	290	3.96:1	0.35	1.03	0.26	1.38
	Sept	1,561	1,188	1.31:1	0.83	0.51	0.38	1.09
	Oct	1,981	2,597	1:1.31	1.36	0.39	0.50	1.04
	Nov	1,118	2,300	1:2.06	2.24	0.30	0.63	1.09
	Dec	2,291	3,987	1:1.74	1.40	0.23	0.39	0.80
1952	Jan	2,451	3,660	1:1.49	1.31	0.14	0.20	0.87
	Feb	2,624	3,591	1:1.37	0.65	0.11	0.15	0.47
	Mar	3,427	2,624	1.31:1	1.08	0.15	0.18	1.41
	Apr	3,870	1,408	2.75:1	1.14	0.36	0.13	3.13
	May	5,151	640	8.05:1	0.66	1.40	0.18	5.31
	Jun	2,883	320	9.01:1	0.73	0.94	0.10	6.56
	July	2,673	448	5.97:1	0.60	0.89	0.15	3.57
	Aug	2,923	1,216	2.40:1	1.09	0.16	0.07	2.63
	Sept	3,649	1,856	1.97:1	1.56	0.54	0.27	3.07
	Oct	4,321	1,344	3.22:1	0.60	0.37	0.12	1.94
	Nov	2,614	1,216	2.15:1	1.03	0.25	0.12	2.22
	Dec	3,557	1,536	2.32:1	0.73	0.07	0.03	1.69
1953	Jan	3,579	1,269	2.82:1	1.09	0.08	0.03	3.07
	Feb	2,936	1,577	1.86:1	0.89	0.13	0.07	1.65
	Mar	3,741	1,995	1.88:1	0.93	0.10	0.05	1.75
	Apr	4,955	1,615	3.07:1	0.48	0.25	0.08	1.49
	May	4,831	1,478	3.27:1	1.18	0.07	0.02	3.86
	Jun	4,210	1,280	3.29:1	1.69	-	-	5.55
	July	3,037	778	3.85:1	0.85	0.25	0.07	3.43
Totals		76,542	40,592	1.89:1	0.99	0.25	0.13	1.86

earlier period, and are any significant trends apparent? Probably the most remarkable thing is that fighter-versus-fighter combat appears to have been safer in the Korean conflict that it was in World War 2. With a few notable exceptions the loss ratios per 100 sorties are well down, while victory ratios are not high by comparison. The range of force ratios is wider, with the USAF achieving advantages of eight and 9:1 in the early summer of 1952, and while this huge force disparity achieved better results than (with one exception) at any other time, it was hardly decisive; the communist forces losing only about six percent during this period. In fact, the most successful period for the USAF came in May and June 1953, when they claimed a total of 128 victories for a single loss at an average force ratio of only 3.57.

One odd trend does emerge; out of the fifty victory ratio results, five out of the top seven were gained in the face of adverse force ratios, one of them at odds of 8:1 against. This trend confirms one that was apparent in the Second World War although to a lesser degree; that an out-numbered force tends to inflict a higher loss ratio on its larger opponent. On the other hand, it must be admitted that the 8:1 disparity also saw the third worst loss ratio out of the fifty as well as the third best victory ratio.

What can we reasonably conclude from these figures? Firstly, that force counts in the long run most of the time although it demonstrably has far less effect in a single engagement, which can go either way, regardless of the force ratios involved. Secondly that it does not always count even in a protracted campaign. Thirdly that other factors must be present which have a greater effect. What are these other factors, and what effect do they have?

No two opposing airplanes perform exactly alike, and it would be very rare in a war situation to find one type that was superior to its opponent in every deparfment. A better fighter is undoubtedly an advantage to its pilot, but the advantage has historically been marginal at best. This point will be addressed at length in the following chapters, with a look into the future. Tactics and teamwork play a large part in success or failure, victory or defeat. Tactics is arguably the major factor in a protracted campaign, as well as often being decisive in isolated engagements, while teamwork enhances the effectiveness of the flying unit in action, making it far better than the sum of its constituent parts. Finally there is pilot quality, and this is the most decisive factor of all. As we have seen, this materially affected the outcomes of several Second World War campaigns, and there can be little doubt that it was the main factor in MiG Alley. Let us have a closer look.

On average the USAF flew just over 100 sorties for each

victory claimed, while the communist forces flew about 400 sorties for each USAF fighter lost. As noted before, this does not look very dangerous to the participants; it also looks very difficult for individual pilots to run up a score. The normal tour of operations in the theater was 100 missions; although some pilots came back a second time. The odds on any particular pilot knocking down just one MiG-15 during his tour of duty was slightly less than a stone-bonking certainty, it was quite possible to fly the hundred missions without scoring, and a surprisingly high proportion of Sabre pilots did just that. On the other hand, Korea, like every other air war, produced a handful of pilots who beat the odds. They were very few in number; just eight Sabre pilots accounted for a total of 98 MiGs. Less than one percent of the Sabre pilots scored thirteen percent of the total victories. Further down the scale, the 39 aces of the conflict notched up no less than 287 scalps between them; less than five percent of Sabre pilots accounted for 38 percent of the total victories.

What is the value of the aces? To assess this we must wander into the realms of theory. All we know for certain is that they are the spearhead of the fighter force, but their value must go far beyond a mere number of enemy aircraft destroyed. If, as a purely theoretical exercise we removed these men from the conflict, what would the result have been? The effect on the overall force ratios would have been absolutely marginal. The drop in the exchange ratio would have been dramatic, from 7.5:1 down to 4.6:1, a reduction of nearly forty percent. Take away their example and their leadership, and morale and fighting effectiveness would have been reduced, by an amount that is unquantifiable; while at the same time the morale and effectiveness of their opponents might easily have been higher than it was, which is also an unknown factor. All that can be said with any certainty is that the exchange ratio would have slumped still further, with consequent effects on both the victory and loss ratios. It cannot be denied that this small band of successful pilots affected the outcome of the air war in a manner out of all proportion to their numbers.

MiG Alley is not the only campaign in which this happened. It is simply typical. This same sort of ratio keeps cropping up; five percent of pilots accounting for about forty percent of their foes, and inspiring their comrades by example while increasing their fighting effectiveness by leadership and knowledge. Perhaps the only major air campaign in which this has not happened was Vietnam, which produced only two American pilot aces in the course of the conflict, although it is believed that a handful of North Vietnamese pilots achieved the magic "five." From the American point of view, Vietnam was "different," and we shall come to this in due course.

The dream of an air force commander is to have a fighter force entirely composed of pilots with the magic ingredient, "the ace factor." In a democratic society this is totally impossible as there are simply not enough to go around. In a totalitarian state it might just be possible; as the entire young male population would be available, in theory at any rate. Many aces of the past came from civilian life, in which they had no thought of flying fighters. Only the urgency of war plucked them from obscurity and placed them in the spotlight. The longing to fly in peacetime is not enough, and many potential aces slip the net.

The next best thing would be to have sufficient pilots with ace potential to spread evenly among the fighter squadrons. As we have seen, just one or two per unit would increase the combat effectiveness of that unit immeasurably. The difficulty lies in the selection process. As defense analyst Pierre Sprey once said, "combat is the ultimate, and the unkindest judge." Once the shooting starts, the aces will emerge, but this is far too late in the day. Ideally, selection should be carried out even before pilot training begins. The difficulty lies in knowing who to select. It has long been held that aces are born and not made. There is a large element of truth in this, but it is not the whole story. If the potential can be identified, it can be sharpened and honed by knowledge and training. It is noticeable that in any war, certain units are far more successful than others. In terms of cold figures, they contain more than their share of aces. It is also easy to establish that they are better led. Perhaps the classic examples come from the First World War, with Boelke's Jagdstaffel 2 and Richthofen's Jagdstaffel

11, or on the Allied side, No. 56 and No. 74 Squadrons of the RFC and the RAF. It can be argued that good leadership and personal example made the most of the potential that was latent in the pilots.

To discover the ace factor, we must search through the historical records and attempt to quantify the attributes that made the top scoring pilots great. In order to do this properly we must set the scene. Information taken out of context is valueless. The ace factor is part inborn and part learned. From time to time great fighter pilots have set down rules of combat in order to help the less gifted survive long enough to learn. These must also be examined, as they give an insight into the way that the aces think. They are also valuable in that they give an impression of the nature of fighter combat at the time that they were drawn up. It is perhaps surprising that many of even the oldest rules still have relevance today. It has already been stated that situational awareness is *the* ace factor; there are still other factors, and these will not be neglected along the way.

Chapter 2

The Great War in the Air

At the outbreak of the First World War, the airplane was widely regarded as an unreliable toy which might or might not have some value in the reconnaissance role. Some experiments were carried out prior to the outbreak of hostilities, but these generally only served to either confirm or deny the preconceived ideas of the pro or anti airplane factions. Fortunately there were enough of the former to make converts among the uncommitted, and the airplane was gradually accepted as a legitimate and useful tool of the army, not only for reconnaissance, but as an artillery spotter and a possible means of carrying the war into the enemy's rear areas. From this point, the next step was obvious. The enemy had to be prevented from carrying out these functions in his turn; airplanes would therefore have to be capable of fighting each other. The problem was how?

With hindsight, it seems obvious that the weapon most suited to the fighting airplane, or scout, as they were soon to become known, was the machine-gun. The trouble was that machine-guns with their ammunition supply were heavy, and could easily add between ten and fifteen percent to the empty weight of the scout. In the days when power loadings often exceeded 15 or even 20 lb. for each horsepower produced by the engine, the weight and drag of a single gun could adversely affect the aircraft's performance to a considerable degree. The Vickers Company equipped their FB5 Gunbus with a Maxim machine-gun as early as 1913, as a private venture, but the result was a scout that could barely manage 70 mph on the level, and had a poor rate of climb. Assuming that the Gunbus could reach the altitude of an opponent in the time available, it could only fight if the opponent also wanted to fight; it could only force battle on the enemy if that enemy was willing to accept the challenge. Another problem of this period was that a second crewman was needed to operate the machine-gun, thereby adding even more weight and drag, and further reducing performance.

Many exotic weapons were proposed; from bombs and grenades to grapnells (a German aircraft was actually brought down in this manner by an aircraft of the Imperial Russian Air Service), through blunderbusses (proposed by a Royal Flying Corps pilot and actually recorded as being used by a French flyer against German ace Oswald Boelcke), to the more obvious and not very effective pistols and repeating carbines.

Equally troublesome was the manner in which the weapons should be employed. Many theorists of the day who saw clearly that the firepower afforded by a machine-gun was the only reasonable option felt that the best solution would be to use a large, multi-engined aircraft with more than one gunner, their conception of an air fight being two machines sailing along side by side exchanging broadsides in a manner reminiscent of a naval action between warships. Pioneer British aviators Claude Grahame-White and Harry Harper reasoned that taking a position above an opponent while armed with a revolver would give a decisive advantage.

> "... it placed at a clear disadvantage the aviator who found himself beneath. While his opponent could fire down on him, as he sat exposed in his machine, he himself, reduced to the necessity of facing upwards—no easy position from which to aim a weapon—could see very little of his adversary, owing to the fact that the hull of the latter's machine, lying between him and a weapon fired from below, not only protected him (the upper man) to a certain extent from a bullet, but made it difficult for the man beneath to place a shot with any accuracy."

Both of these methods make one totally unwarranted assumption, that the opponent is simply going to sit there and be shot at. They are quoted only to show how little anyone really knew about air fighting. The assumption that a revolver could be a lethal weapon in the air combat arena is also incredible to

The Sopwith Pup, as flown by Arthur Gould Lee and Leonard Rochford in France, 1917. A delight to fly, its performance was insufficient to allow its pilots to force combat on the heavier but faster German scouts. Close examination reveals that the fabric to the upper wing center section has been removed to give the pilot a view forwards and upwards. (FLYPAST)

us today, although the idea seemed sensible enough at the time the words were written. The fact of the matter is that no one had any idea of the form that air fighting would take. It was a blank canvas which could only be filled up into a complete picture by hard-won and often lethal experience. Of all the theorists, only F.W. Lanchester came up with something really relevant when he stated that an altitude advantage represented a store of potential energy which could be used to outmaneuver an enemy. This remarkable piece of prophecy dates from October 1914, and has been the keynote of fighter tactics until very recent times.

During the first few months of the war, the combatants were not too dangerous to each other. Occasional victories were scored using rifles or carbines, but there was little method and much luck in the few successful combats. Machine-guns began increasingly to be carried by two-seaters, operated by the observer, who was usually but not always seated behind the pilot. These were not very effective. The field of fire was poor, shooting forward being severely constrained by the wings and the propeller disc. To the sides was better, although the elevation obtainable was restricted, while the depression was even more so. Unless an opponent could be found who was willing to fly alongside exchanging shots there was little chance of success, although the better performing airplane did at least stand a chance of taking up a favorable position which hampered the return fire of the opposing gunner. On the other hand, the machine-guns of the day were not all that accurate. Fixed in a clamp on the sighting range they could produce a reasonable grouping, but fired from a less than rigid mounting on a vibrating airplane, with the gunner trying to overcome the buffetting of the slipstream (which, incidentally, affected him as well as the gun), while solving the problems of range estimation, lead, bullet drop, and probably target precession at times, not to mention bullet trail, the gun did little more than spray the general area of sky towards which it was pointing. Aiming to the rear was better, although not by much, but it was asking rather a lot of the target aircraft to follow along while being shot at and unable to shoot back. Accurate shooting problems apart, it was close to impossible to handle the airplane in an aggressive manner using only a swiveling gun mounted to the rear.

The only possible solution to this was a fixed forward-firing machine-gun pointing along the line of flight. The mounting could be much more rigid, although nothing could be done to prevent the vibration of the aircraft, while there was no slipstream buffetting at the firer to upset his aim. Many of the aiming problems remained, but the fixed forward-firing gun was inherently more accurate than the swivel-mounted version. There were three ways by which this gun location might be achieved. The first was to find some way of shooting through the propeller without shooting it off. The second was to mount the gun in such a way that it fired outside the propeller disc. The third way was to utilize an aircraft layout in which the propeller was not in the line of fire. All of these were tried more or less simultaneously. Of them, the first was found to be the most satisfactory; the line of fire was aligned more or less with the axis of the machine, it lent itself well to belt feeding, which meant that reloading did not have to be

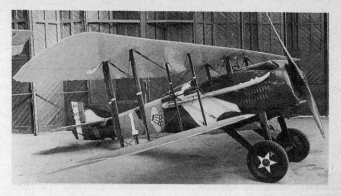

The Spad VII as flown by Guynemer and other French aces. This "grim-looking scout," as Cecil Lewis described it, was very tough, and well suited to the dive and zoom tactics used on the Western Front. This particular example has been painted to represent a Spad XIII of the American 94th Aero Pursuit Squadron flown by top-scoring ace Eddie Rickenbacker. (FLYPAST)

accomplished so often as with a drum-fed gun, while the mounting could be really solid. It had two drawbacks. An interrupter, or synchronization gear had to be fitted to prevent the bullets damaging the propeller. This slowed the rate of fire by an appreciable amount, typically from 600 to 450 rounds per minute, while it could go wrong, with disastrous results.

The second method involved mounting the gun on the upper wing center section. The ammunition supply was carried in a drum holding either 48 or 97 bullets; running out of ammunition in the middle of a fight was an ever-present hazard, while changing the drum involved flying "hands-off" for a few seconds, during which time the pilot was distracted by his task and vulnerable to a surprise attack. The mounting was more susceptible to vibration than the first type, while the final problem involved aiming. With the gun mounted appreciably higher than the sight, the pilot had either to learn to aim slightly low, or else to harmonize both gun and sight at a fixed range, which was the most usual course. At anything other than the harmonized range, aiming was therefore inaccurate, the amount varying according to the distance variationfrom the optimum range.

The third was, from a shooting point of view, by far the best. The mounting could be solid and there was no reduction in the rate of fire, while the gun could be aligned along the axis of the aircraft. Unfortunately this could only be done by adopting the "pusher" aircraft configuration, with the engine mounted behind the pilot. With this layout, the tail surfaces had to be carried on booms passing on each side of the propeller, which were of a lattice construction and which caused very high drag, as a direct consequence of which, the aircraft performance suffered considerably.

The French were the first to introduce the ace system, and lionized their successful scout pilots, likening them to the heroes of legend such as Roland de Roncevalles. The British took the opposite view and sought unsuccessfully to suppress personal publicity, while the Germans took a more middle course, stating that ten victories was the minimum number of victories needed to qualify rather than the five of the French. This ruling also applied to the Austro-Hungarian Empire. When America entered the war, their close links with the French flying service led them to adopt the five victory ace system. In all, something over 1,500 pilots scored more than four victories, and were thus elevated, officially or otherwise, to ace status.

More than half of the aces came from the British Empire flying services; the RFC, RNAS, and after April 1, 1918, the RAF. Germany followed with 363; France had about 160, and the USA could count a total of 110, although a considerable number of these achieved their scores while flying with French or British units. German victories were the most rigidly regulated, but as the vast majority of the action took place on their side of the front lines, crashed aircraft could be more easily confirmed. The French were a bit more liberal, counting shared victories as whole scores, while the British were the most easy going of all, although every attempt was made to confirm claims where possible.

Complete accuracy is, of course, impossible. What constitutes a valid claim is a vexed question. Many aircraft of all nations have arrived back at base with a dying pilot, or too badly shot about ever to fly again. On the other hand, there have been many cases where an aircraft has gone down apparently finished that has been recovered. The system of count-

The controversy of performance versus maneuverability was never entirely conclusive in World War 1, many of the leading German aces, notably the elder Richthofen and Werner Voss preferring the slower but handier Fokker Dr. 1 Triplane to the speedy Albatros DV. The triplane combined a lot of lifting area with a high aspect ratio but a short span. (FLYPAST)

ing scores has many drawbacks, but it also has its virtues. It lifts the morale of the civilian population; all generations need heroes. It also boosts the morale of the flyers concerned, while giving a numerical value to the most successful acts as a spur to the other pilots in the unit. Many of the early aces were held up as an example to younger pilots, to whom they acted as an inspiration.

The preponderance of British aces does not stem from their liberal attitude to claims by more than a slight degree. Their losses were equally high, and for most of the war they faced the cream of the Luftstreitkrafte. The fighting was almost invariably harder on the British front, as can be deduced by the fact that *all* of Manfred von Richthofen's eighty victories were scored against them. Nor did the aggressive British policy of carrying the fight to the enemy make for an easy time. By contrast, the French tended to be less offensively minded, while the Germans were outnumbered by a fair margin

The majority of top aces in the Royal Flying Corps and later the Royal Air Force, gained a high proportion of their victories in the high performance SE 5a. (FLYPAST)

throughout the entire period of hostilities, and could not afford the losses bound to ensure through operating over hostile territory for much of the time. In fact, the British and the German air services had more aces mainly because any pilot who managed to survive the critical first ten missions had more opportunities; both sides operated in a "target rich" environment.

It would be a fruitless exercise to attempt to examine and analyze the entire ace spectrum, as it would be repetitious to say the least. The best that we can do is to pick out some of the best known and documented pilots, and compare their records with a handful of the lesser known whose diaries and recollections have been preserved for posterity, in order to obtain a spread of experiences. If, for example we were to draw a "cut" line at twenty victories, we should still have more than enough information. For example, the British forces contained some 66 (out of many thousands) pilots who scored twenty or more victories. Their total was no less than 2,077, giving an average of 31½ each. France had just fourteen aces who scored twenty or more, who accounted for a total of 467 victories for an average of 33½ each. German pilots with twenty or more victories totalled 72 sharing 2,210 victories at an average of 30½ each. Of the minor combatants, Belgium had Willy Coppens with 34, although 33 of these were kite balloons; the USA had just two, of whom Frank Luke was primarily a balloon buster also; Austria-Hungary had four with 115 shared for an average of 29 each, while Italy had five with a total of 127 and an average of 25½ each.

The remarkable thing about these figures is the evenness of spread in this sample of the higher scorers. There is no really marked national predominance among the major powers, patriotic prejudice notwithstanding. The only real variance is in the proportion of major to minor aces, where the British sample is just under ten percent; the French sample is slightly less at nine percent, while the German sample shows more than double, at just less than twenty percent. The USA shows up poorly against these figures, but it must be remembered that not only were they only in the war for the last few months as an effective force, but a handful of American pilots achieved high scores while flying with the British, which would even things up a bit. Why is the German figure twice as high as the others? Outnumbered and flying mainly over friendly territory, they not only had more opportunities to score, but had a better chance of surviving as combatants. A British pilot, perhaps wounded, or maybe nursing a shot-up engine, often had no choice but to land in enemy territory and become a guest of the Kaiser for the duration. For German pilots, this was far less likely, and even if caught over Allied lines, the prevailing wind was mostly in their favor.

There is one other factor which must be taken into consideration at this point. It is arguable that German leadership, insofar as the purely air war went, was better than that of the Allies, at least at fighting unit level. The Germans were often criticized for not taking risks. In this respect, they fought a far more professional war than either the British, who confused it with huntin', shootin' and fishin', and the French, who romanticized it. It is certainly true that no other nation produced a tactician of the stature of Boelcke, who has gone down in history as the father of air fighting, or anyone remotely approaching him. Boelcke's influence pervaded the German fighter arm throughout the entire war, his pupils, of whom Manfred von Richthofen was the most famous, carrying on his teachings after his death.

Air fighting proper started with Frenchman Roland Garros in early 1915. Frustrated by not being able to shoot forward, and unable to obtain a workable interrupter gear, he had steel deflectors fitted to his propeller to protect it from bullets which otherwise would have hit it. His first victory came on April 1, his victim being the two-seater reconnaissance aircraft of Leutnant von Waxheim, which he picked out of a formation of four machines, all of which were unarmed except for pistols. This was followed by three further victories in quick succession, which shook the morale of the German air units in that region. Garros' luck was not to last. Just nineteen days after his first victory, the engine of his Morane Saulnier L failed as he was attacking a ground target, and he was forced to land in German-held territory, watched, by one of those strange coincidences that occur more often than generally credited, by Ernst Udet, who was to end the war as Germany's ranking ace. Garros' secret was out, and within a matter of days, the Germans had gone one better and fitted a synchronization gear to a Fokker monoplane, enabling it also to shoot through the propeller disc. The deflector plates soldiered on for a while in French service, Eugene Gilbert scoring five and Adolphe Pegoud six victories during the summer of 1915 in their Morane-Saulnier Ns before they both went down, but the deflector plate idea was at best a makeshift, as it reduced propeller efficiency, and with it performance, by a considerable amount, while the shock of bullets hitting the plates put an irregular strain on the engine. But the way had been shown, and air combat could now begin properly.

For the fighter pilot, the problems fall into three main categories; what he can see, what he can do with his aircraft, and what he can hit with his armament. Dealing with these in turn, a man with good vision on a clear day can pick out a biplane of the First World War type and size from about three miles away, although recognition would normally not be possible from much more than two miles. In hazy conditions these distances would be much less, although if the other airplane was outlined against a bright cloud, they might be rather more. If the other airplane was below the horizon, it would be more difficult to see. Relative movement also plays a part. If it is approaching from head-on or tail-on, or flying a similar course at a similar speed, it will be more difficult to see than if it is flying at, say, right angles. Formations can be seen at greater distances, while a large dogfight could often be picked out from six to eight miles away. Unfortunately, large areas of the sky are blanked out by the engine, wings, fuselage and tail of the fighter, while the pilot can only search in one direction at a time. Clouds often obstruct vision, while the sun casts a blinding dazzle in a cone roughly fifteen degrees wide, in which little or nothing can be seen.

The aircraft that the pilot is flying also has limitations; the obvious ones of maximum speed, rate of climb, and ceiling, and some not so obvious, such as rate of turn, acceleration, and how quickly it can begin a turn, climb, or dive. To the uninitiated, it always appears that the fighter has unlimited maneuver options, but in practice it does not work out like this. What it has is called an energy state, which has always existed but was not conceptualized until the 1960s, and of which more later. The energy state is a combination of the kinetic energy contained in the aircraft as it flies, plus the positional energy given by altitude, which had already been stated by Lanchester, and which simply means that altitude can be converted into speed by means of a dive. Both climbing and hard maneuver tend to result in a loss of speed, and the lower the speed drops, the less the fighter can do by way of maneuver. Below stalling speed the fighter can no longer fly, while at just above the stall, it is unable to climb, and can perform only the gentlest of turns unless it is prepared to lose altitude to gain the extra energy necessary. Unless its speed in the fight is kept high, it is a sitting duck, unable to maneuver offensively, and predictable defensively in that it can only dive away.

Finally, the pilot has the problem of what he can reasonably expect to hit with his armament. The aircraft of the First World War were small by today's standards, and while a marksman on a ground range could expect to score a respect-

able number of hits on a similarly sized static target at between 500 and 600 yards, using the machine-guns of the
period, hitting a moving target from an unstable and vibrating
airplane at less than half this distance was virtually impossible. Nor was it enough just to perforate the machine; many
aircraft returned safely although riddled with bullets. Barring
the occasional lucky hit on something structurally important;
the engine, the pilot or the fuel tank had to be damaged to
stand any chance of downing an opponent, and even then this
could not be absolutely guaranteed to do the job. The size of
the vulnerable area was very small indeed, and more than one
hit was often needed to finish the job. For this reason crossing
shots at high angles of deflection were rarely successful, even
when used by the most gifted marksman, as the bullets tended
to be spread along the length of the target, rather than
grouped. The most reliable method was to get in close for a
small or no-deflection shot.

All these things had to be discovered by the early fighter
pilots, almost entirely by trial and error, in the unforgiving
arena of air combat. How they fared, we shall see during our
quest for the Clue Bird of SA. They were engaged in a quest
of their own, with no rules or guidance. Just a handful were
successful, using a mixture of courage, aggression, caution,
and instinct. Four of them became famous far beyond the
confines of their own service, or even their own country. They
were the Germans Max Immelmann and Oswald Boelcke, the
Englishman Albert Ball, and the Frenchman Georges Guynemer. Not one survived the war, but between them they set an
example that inspired flyers of all nations and all periods.

The Fokker Menace, 1915–1916

The Fokker Eindecker, equipped with one, and later two machine-guns firing through the propeller disc, was destined to
have a far-reaching effect on air combat, and enabled the
Luftstreitkrafte to attain a measure of superiority for several
months. Its performance was nothing startling. The E III,
which was the most used type, could manage a top speed of
87 mph at sea level, with a ceiling of 11,500 ft., and took half

an hour to reach 10,000 ft. Wing loading was 7.76 lb/ft^2 and power loading was 13.42 lb/hp. It was, however, as good as or better than the aircraft by which it was at first opposed, and could be dived at a steep angle without shedding its wings, which was not always the case with aircraft in those days. Typical of its opponents was the Vickers FB5, a two-seater pusher biplane with a top speed of only 70 mph, a ceiling of 9,000 ft., and which took nineteen minutes to struggle up to 6,500 ft. At 5.37 lb/ft^2, its wing loading was better than that of its German opponent, but its power loading of 20.5 lb/hp was much worse.

So far as is known, the first operational flight by an Eindecker was made on June 24, 1915, with Oswald Boelcke at the controls. At this point in the war, there were no fighting squadrons as such, just small units of two or three aircraft tasked with protecting the artillery spotters. At first very few Fokkers were available, and they tended to stay on their own side of the lines, but Boelcke commented in a letter home in mid-July, "the consequence is that they do nothing but go for joyrides round our lines, and never get a shot at the enemy, whereas I have the pleasure of getting a good smack at the fellows over yonder. One must not wait till they come across, but seek them out and hunt them down."

Oswald Boelcke, the German aviator who scored forty victories against the British and French forces before dying in a mid-air crash with one of his own men in 1916. (RAF MUSEUM, HENDON)

In spite of this aggressive attitude, chances were few, and it was not until August 23 that Boelcke managed a decisive combat in his new single-seater, firing a few shots at a Bristol Scout, which later landed in its own lines. Max Immelmann had meanwhile opened his score some three weeks earlier by wounding the pilot of a British BE2c which was forced to land behind the German lines. After this, the pace increased a bit, and by January 1916, both Boelcke and Immelmann had raised their scores to eight each, at which point they were awarded Germany's highest decoration, the Pour le Mérite, or Blue Max. By the standards of later times, this progress seems painfully slow, but it should be remembered that the two young Germans were pioneers in their field, and had to find the best methods by trial and error. They had often flown together, and it has been suggested that this was the origin of a fighting pair, working as a team. There seems to be little enough evidence that this was the case, and it is far more probable that they flew together for mutual support against the Allied formations that were coming into use at this time, rather than trying to operate as a team. Later on, Fokkers usually hunted in pairs, but this generally consisted of an experienced pilot showing a novice the ropes, rather than an organized team. Seven-victory ace Max von Mulzer was a pupil of Immelmann's in this way.

Immelmann's main claim to fame lies in the famous turn that bears his name. In essence, it consists of a fast, diving attack followed by a zoom climb, ruddering over the top, then aileron-turning on the way back down to line up for another pass. He seems to have been the first pilot to consistently use the vertical plane for maneuver, rather than the horizontal turn, and his discovery of it would appear to have been instinctive rather than reasoned. While it was very successful, it needed excellent timing and judgement of distance to achieve results, although the record does appear to show that the Immelmann Turn made a greater impression on the RFC flyers on the receiving end, than on the German Air Service users. It reached the stage where every Fokker encountered was believed to be Immelmann; Boelcke flew more often against the French during this period, and was not as well known to the British.

Stemming from this period was a sort of reverse situational awareness among the British flyers. The Eindecker was credited with being able to outpace, outclimb and outmaneuver any aircraft in RFC service by a goodly margin. It was some sort of superfighter that had the beating of any Allied type. This impression arose from a combination of relatively heavy losses in air combat (which could hardly have been anything else, air combat losses up to this time having been negligible), and subjective judgement; for example, future high-scoring ace James McCudden, flying as an NCO observer in a Morane Parasol described it as "a long dark brown form fairly streaking across the sky" and "when it got above and behind our middle machine it dived on to it for all the world like a huge hawk on a hapless sparrow." Judgements and descriptions such as these did nothing for morale, which reached a low ebb. Even those who repelled an attack, and there were many of them, tended to recount their adventures as an epic escape from mortal danger. Had the truth been known earlier, morale would have been far better, with crews having far more will to fight back, whereas they were often hacked down as they attempted to escape.

It is interesting that Boelcke makes no reference to the Immelmann Turn, although it can hardly be doubted that he noted any maneuvers that were likely to bring success. His own learning curve proceeded apace. On October 16 he was attacked by a French Voisin, which approached from the front quarter. He commented, "I calmly let him fire away, for the combined speed of two opponents meeting one another reduces the chance of a hit to practically nil—as I have already found by frequent experience . . . it is absolutely essential to fly in such a way that your adversary cannot shoot at you, if you can manage it." Closing to between 25 and fifty yards, he pumped 200 shots into the French machine, which fell away vertically and crashed into a plantation. On December 29 he joined in a scrap between Immelmann and two British aircraft. As is often the case, the encounter turned into two one-versus-one combats, and a whirling, turning dogfight developed, during which over 3,000 ft. of altitude was lost, and although Boelcke damaged his opponent, he ran out of ammunition. While he continued to make dummy attacks to confuse the English flyer, Immelmann entered the fray, having disposed of his own opponent, but suffered a gun jam almost straight away. Although forced down to ground level, the British machine managed to escape across the lines.

The lesson of this combat was taken to heart by the young German flyer, and during a similar combat on January 14, 1916, he deliberately conserved his ammunition, firing only when his sight were definitely "on." For several minutes of maneuver fighting, he did not fire a single shot. At last an opportunity presented itself, and a well-aimed burst put the engine of the British machine out of action. With no power, it force-landed between the trench lines. The British observer had done a considerable amount of shooting back, and Boelcke also force-landed as a result of this encounter with his fuel tank riddled and a bullet hole in his sleeve.

Oswald Boelcke was already emerging as an analytical thinker and theoretician as well as a fighting pilot, and from November 1915 he had begun to send reports on tactics, organization and equipment direct to headquarters, bypassing the usual formal channels. This is what began to set him apart from Max Immelmann, with whom he conducted a friendly rivalry in the field as to who would be the leading scorer. Both men had a technical and mechanical bent, but Boelcke appears to have been much more aware of what was going on in the sky around him, and more importantly, why. One of his technical reports has been recorded. The Eindecker had been continually upgraded until it reached the E.IV variant, which had an engine of double the power of the original E.I and E.II types. It carried two machine-guns angled up from the aircraft axis at fifteen degrees. While Max Immelmann used the E.IV successfully, Boelcke was not very impressed. He commented that the E.IV was too slow and lost too much speed in the climb, while the rate of climb fell off rapidly at heights above 10,000 ft. Maneuver was poor, due to the adverse effects of the torque caused by the large rotary engine, and his opinion was that the upward angle of the guns was unsuitable for combat. While Immelmann went on to use the E.IV with no less than three machine-guns fitted, trading performance and maneuverability for firepower, Boelcke was pleased to revert to his E.III model, which he considered to be a more suitable fighting vehicle.

This total absorption with all aspects of air combat was molding him into not only a great fighter ace, but arguably the greatest fighter leader of all time, and certainly the most influential, often referred to as "the father of air fighting." If the case seems overstated, consider that when his fighting career started, combat between aircraft was a haphazard affair, with the contestants knowing only what they wanted to do but having little or no idea how to achieve it, and ended less than eighteen months later as the result of a flying accident having put air combat onto a scientific footing, using formations rather than individuals, his legacy being a set of rules for air fighting that needs little amendment for use in the jet age. He put his own theories into practice, and died as Germany's ranking ace. It can be truly said that Boelcke laid the foundations on which fighter pilots of all other nations built.

Meanwhile, the Allies had been taking steps to counter the Fokker menace. The first fighting scout squadrons were formed, arriving at the front from February 1916 onwards. They consisted of three main types. The British Airco DH 2 was a single-seat pusher biplane armed with a single Lewis gun. It could reach 93 mph at sea level, had a service ceiling of 14,000 ft., and could climb to 6,500 ft. in just twelve minutes. Wing loading was 5.8 lb/ft^2, and power loading 13.2 lb/hp. In absolute performance terms it had only a marginal edge over the E.III, but was far more maneuverable. The FE 2b was a two seater pusher with a performance roughly comparable to the DH 2, while the Nieuport Scout was a single-seat tractor biplane armed with a single Lewis gun mounted on the top wing and firing over the propeller disc. It had a maximum speed of 107 mph, a ceiling of 17,400 ft., and could reach an altitude of 10,000 ft. in nine minutes. Wing loading was 7.7 lb/ft^2, and power loading only 11.2 lb/hp. The two British pushers held an edge over the Fokker, but the French-built Nieuport simply outclassed it. Encouraged by their new machines, the British in particular started to carry the fight to the enemy.

Meanwhile Boelcke was mainly engaged with the French.

The "office area" of the Bristol F2b, showing clearly the Aldis telescopic sight. With his eye glued to this, the pilot had little awareness of what was going on around him, but he had the observer to both warn him and guard his tail with the ring-mounted twin Lewis guns. (FLYPAST)

His seventeenth victory came on May 21, 1916. He described it in a letter home thus:

"Two Nieuports were flying at a great height on the far side of their lines, but I did not attack them . . . then I saw two Caudrons that had hitherto escaped my notice wandering about below. When I went for one of them and began to shoot, I saw one of the Nieuports diving down on me . . . I broke away from the Caudrons and bore northwards, with the Nieuport behind me in the belief that I had failed to notice him. I kept a sharp eye on him until he was within two hundred meters of me—then I suddenly went into a turn and flew at him . . . he wrenched his machine around and bolted southward." The French pilot then did the wrong thing; he flew straight, giving Boelcke an easy shot from 100 meters astern. He was seen to crash by the German infantry.

This combat contains several interesting points. First is Boelcke's disinclination to attack the Nieuports from a position of disadvantage. Second is the fact that Boelcke at first overlooked the Caudrons which were below, possibly because he was more concerned with danger from above. Third is that even when shooting at a Caudron, an activity which takes every ounce of concentration, Boelcke was still able to remain aware of the potential threat posed by the two Nieuports, and react as soon as one made a move against him. Fourth, he was able to present to the French pilot a picture of the situation as it was not, the Frenchman thought that he had the advantage of surprise, and appears to have been totally disconcerted when he discovered that this was not the case, so disconcerted in fact, that he made an elementary error and paid the supreme price. Boelcke was fully master of the situation at all times, whereas the French pilot only thought that he was.

The increasing use of French aircraft in large formations led to the need to counter them in strength. In June, Boelcke formed the first Jagdstaffel, or fighting squadron, at Sivry, on the Verdun front. It was not a regular formation, but can be regarded as the forerunner of the units that were formed the following August and September. He was then overtaken by events, the first of which was the death of Immelmann on June 18. As is often the case, accounts were conflicting. Immelmann went down during a fight between four Fokkers of the Douai unit, and seven FE 2bs of No. 25 Squadron, RFC. German accounts state that Immelmann's interrupter gear failed and he shot his own propeller off, which caused other damage leading to a fatal crash, while RFC records credit Corporal Waller, the gunner in the FE 2b flown by Lieutenant McCubbin, as having shot him down. Either way, Immelmann was now out of the battle, with a final score of fifteen, three behind Boelcke.

The loss of Immelman was a great blow to the Luftstreitkrafte, coming as it did at a time when command of the air was rapidly passing to the Allies. As a direct result, Boelcke was grounded, and a few days later he was sent to the East to observe the scene. Before he left, he composed, at the behest of *Flugfeldchef* Colonel Thomsen, his famous rules for air fighting, the so-called Dicta Boelcke. More than one version of these rules has appeared, and it seems that they may later have been embellished a little. The following is the version given by Colonel Thomsen to Professor Johannes Werner for the preparation of the book *Knight of Germany*.

1) Try to secure advantages before attacking. If possible, keep the sun behind you.
2) Always carry through an attack when you have started it.
3) Fire only at close range, and only when your opponent is properly in your sights.
4) Always keep your eye on your opponent, and never let yourself be deceived by ruses.
5) In any form of attack it is essential to assail your opponent from behind.
6) If your opponent dives on you, do not try to evade his onslaught, but fly to meet it.
7) When over the enemy's lines never forget your own line of retreat.
8) For the Staffel: attack on principle in groups of four or six. When the fight breaks up into a series of single combats, take care that several do not go for one opponent.

Reading between the lines, we can see a determined but cautious pilot, prepared to do everything in his power to load the dice in his favor. The rules themselves are simplistic, and obviously intended for the guidance of a novice. The "advantages before attacking" could have been expanded into a minichapter had Boelcke been so minded, but only the sun is mentioned. In modern times it could have been written as "reduce the enemy's SA!" Rules 2 and 6 are concerned with determination, and could be interpreted as "do not show that your resolve is weakening," and "attack is the best means of defense" respectively. Rules 3 and 5 are concerned with getting results; shooting accurately at close range and with no deflection. The rest are pure situational awareness; do not be deceived, which way is the exit, and do not leave an opponent unengaged because if you do, he may well do some damage through having the time to look around and pick his target while the friendlies are busy ganging up on some poor individual and spending most of their time in keeping out of each other's way. The essence of the whole document can be summed up in two words; "win" and "survive."

Having toured the Balkans and Turkey, Boelcke had reached Kovel, on the Russian front, when he received a telegram recalling him to the West to form one of the new Jagdstaffeln (Jastas for short). This was in mid-August, and by September 2, he was back in action, this time against the British over the Somme battlefield, bringing down a DH 2 flown by Captain Robert Wilson, for his twentieth victory.

It was now Germany's turn to introduce new equipment to reverse the Allied, and particularly the British measure of air superiority. This was done with new biplanes, the Fokker and Halberstadt, and most of all, the Albatros D II scout. Armed with two Spandau machine-guns firing through the propeller disc, the Albatros could top 109 mph, and could get up to around 17,000 ft. Initial climb rate was 3,280 ft. in five minutes. Wing loading was slightly high, at 7.91 lb/ft², which meant that it could not turn with a DH 2, while power loading was good, at 12.21 lb/hp. Against the Nieuport 17 it was very closely matched, with the advantage of a greater weight of firepower. It was with this aircraft that Jasta 2 was mainly equipped, and with which Boelcke would score almost all his further victories.

As pilots and aircraft trickled in, Boelcke launched into a thorough training program, mainly aimed at teamwork. As he stressed over and over, it did not matter who scored the victory as long as the Staffel won it. With a hand-picked bunch of medal-hungry fighter pilots (and whoever heard of a fighter pilot with a small ego?), this was not easy, and seems to have caused him a certain amount of exasperation. He was also the first leader to give what would today be called dissimilar combat training, stressing the weak points of opponent's machines, backed up with practical demonstrations using captured aircraft, and laying down the best methods of dealing with them. For example: the Vickers single-seater (really the DH 2) was noted for losing height during steep turns, al-

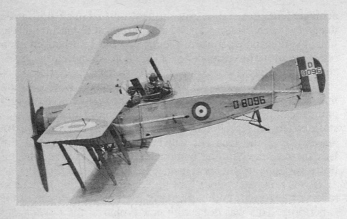

The "Brisfit," as the F2b Bristol Fighter was popularly known, was the First World War equivalent of the Phantom. It was large and powerful, heavily armed, had a two-man crew, and when properly handled could hold its own against smaller and more agile opponents. Entering service in 1917, it was not phased out until 1932; an incredible record for the era. (FLYPAST)

though very agile, and best attacked from behind where the pilot's view was obstructed by the engine; it was also vulnerable to a zoom climb attack from behind and below. The Vickers two-seater (FE 2b) had a limited rearward firing capability, and was to be attacked from the rear, preferably from slightly low. Pilots were cautioned to get on its outside in a turning contest (modern term lag pursuit). The Nieuport was stated as being very fast and agile, but generally lost height as the result of prolonged turning. But in those days, what aircraft didn't?

Jasta 2 commenced operations on September 16, and from then until the end of the month, Boelcke worked them very hard. At the end of the month, a total of 186 sorties had been flown, with 69 engagements and 25 victories, of which the maestro scored ten. Nor was this all; the battlefield had become the classroom, with pre-take-off instruction and an inquest after each engagement. This was a striking achievement, but it was not without loss. Four pilots (one third of the complement) were lost during this period. In the first major engagement, on September 17, Manfred von Richthofen, not yet an ace, but still an experienced flyer, commented on sighting the enemy, "of course, Boelcke was the first to see them, *for he saw more than most men.*" To see first, to be aware of all circumstances, targets and hazards and potentialities, this was the key to the ace pilot.

Previously, Boelcke had scored nineteen victories in roughly ten months, most of them over French aircraft. From here on, all his victories were against British opponents, whose aggressive style gave him plenty of opportunities to score, as well as some rather worrying moments. Over the final eight weeks of his life he added another 21 scalps to his tally, the fortieth and last coming on October 26, just two days before the mid-air collision with one of his own men that ended his life. If it seems that his situational awareness deserted him at the last, this was probably due to fatigue. He had flown intensively over the previous eight weeks, and his final sortie was his sixth that day.

Oswald Boelcke, the man who did so much to make fighter combat a professional activity rather than a sporting pursuit, died at the zenith of his powers. He is the example against whom against all fighter pilots, both aces and leaders, must be judged. What sort of man was he, that could achieve so much?

The surviving records depict him as a calm and balanced character, with few diversions except for going early to bed. He was a disciplinarian, both with himself and with others, of a technical turn of mind, and drank and smoked little. His letters home show that he enjoyed the eminence to which he had risen, and also meeting the highest in the land, although he was openly scornful of blatant publicity. The portrait emerges of a man without weakness, with a wry sense of humor as a saving grace. His face was dominated by the eyes, which were very large and pale blue. Perhaps the closest insights we get were not from his letters home, which were carefully composed not to alarm his parents, but from his star pupil, Manfred von Richthofen, who was recruited for Jasta 2 in Kovel. Richthofen, who incidentally had met Boelcke briefly in October 1915, described it thus:

"I heard a knock on my door early in the morning, and there he stood, a big man wearing the Pour le Mérite." Now Boelcke was not a big man. Photographs show him as being definitely on the short side, as was Richthofen himself. How could Richthofen describe him as big? The answer lies in the personality of the individual, who often gives the observer the impression that he is larger than life. The author has encountered a few cases of this among modern flyers, whose personalities have been such that they seemed to fill and dominate the room they were in, although when viewed objectively later, they proved to be of average height or less, and were not particularly striking in appearance. Richthofen also commented:

"It is strange that everyone who came to know Boelcke imagined that he was his one true friend. I have met about forty of these 'one true' friends of Boelcke's, and each imagined that he indeed was *the* one true friend . . . It was a strange phenomenon that I have observed only in Boelcke. He never had a personal enemy. He was equally friendly to everyone, no more to one, no less to another."

In many ways, Boelcke remains an inscrutable character, just slightly too good to be true. His achievements were undoubtedly the result of natural flair allied to an iron will, which had to overcome the effects of ill-health in addition to the strain of combat, plus a thoughtful and analytical mind. He remains the yardstick against which all successful fighter pilots and fighter leaders should be judged.

The first great ace of the Royal Flying Corps was Albert Ball. Like Boelcke, he was of a mechanical turn of mind, and was short in stature. There the resemblance ends. As a boy, Ball was interested in mechanical gadgets and guns, becoming something of a marksman at an early age. He was probably the most unmilitary figure to achieve great acclaim in the air service of any nation of any period; his letters home deploring the war and the necessity of killing. Unlike the majority of aces, he seems to have become convinced that he would not survive the conflict, and this may have colored his attitude to air fighting, which was hare-brained by comparison with Boelcke's cool and reasoned approach. His main principle was to attack, always regardless of the odds, his sole concession to tactics being to take up a favorable position from which to launch the initial onslaught. Ball was a fighting pilot of great flying ability, but with little inclination to be either fancy or cautious, and certainly never analytical.

His eyesight was exceptional; when once asked how he could tell that very distant aircraft were German, he replied "I smell them." There may have been a germ of truth in this apparently flippant remark, as his fighting was instinctive rather than reasoned. His judgement of speed and distance was outstanding; his preferred method of attack being to close the distance rapidly in a dive past the target, then zoom up from underneath, mushing off speed as he did so, to end almost co-speed with his victim but just below, then pull down the wing-mounted gun of his Nieuport Scout and fire upwards into the belly of his opponent from very close range. Many tried to emulate his methods, but few succeeded; it was far more difficult to perform than it is to describe.

Ball arrived on the Western Front in February 1916, to fly BE 2c artillery spotters with No. 13 Squadron. From the outset he was very aggressive, and was soon transferred to No. 11 Squadron, flying Nieuport single-seaters. While learning the trade he lived dangerously, and while by the following August he had amassed a score surpassing any other RFC pilot, he had been brought down no less than six times himself.

On August 23, 1916 he was transferred to No. 60 Squadron, and his successes continued. While he had to do orthodox patrol and escort work, much of his spare time was spent in lone patrols over the lines, looking for trouble. On August 31 he found it, in the form of a round dozen Roland C IIs over Cambrai. Attacking vertically from above, he forced them to scatter, latching onto one and drilling fifty rounds into its belly from a range of fifteen yards. As it went down to crash, he was engaged in a vicious dogfight with the remainder, and he was forced to evade furiously, taking potshots as opportunity presented. A further Roland fell away out of control, but return fire knocked out the engine of the Nieuport. Out of ammunition and with a dead engine, Ball managed to disengage, firing occasional shots with his automatic, and glided back across the lines. After a rest period, Ball returned to France in April 1917 as a Flight Commander with No. 56 Squadron, flying SE 5s.

Individualistic to the last, he had "personalized" his mount by replacing the original windscreen, removing the synchronized Vickers gun, adding slightly more fuel capacity, and fitting slimmer wheels to reduce drag. He had a second Lewis gun fixed to fire down through the cockpit floor, sighted through a clear panel, although what he hoped to achieve with this is unclear. Later this was removed, and a Vickers mounted along the engine cowling.

By this time, formations were very widely used, and teamwork was becoming the order of the day, but Ball carried on where he had left off tactically the previous year. He went down finally on May 7, 1917 at the end of a long and hard-fought patrol, under mysterious circumstances. His aircraft was seen to fall out of low cloud in an inverted position, and crash behind the German lines. Examination showed that it had not been hit, and although the victory was later awarded to Lothar von Richthofen, with whom he had undoubtedly been engaged, it seems most likely that exhausted after a long and arduous series of fights, he became disoriented in cloud and lost control. His final score was 44.

Ball was not a great tactical thinker, neither was he a leader, and he took little part in squadron life on the ground. He was regarded as a little odd by many, living in a hut on the airfield around which he cultivated a garden. He is recorded as amusing himself in the evenings by lighting a red flare, then walking around it in his pajamas, playing the violin, although a little exaggeration may have crept in here. His value lay in the example he set, which inspired others, and showed them what could be achieved. His SA must have been good to achieve as many successful attacks as he did, and also to survive as long as he did, although a strong element of luck aided him in this.

The cavalier French pilot, Georges Guynemer, who was shot down in September with a final score of fifty-three. (POPPERFOTO)

The French equivalent to Ball was Georges Guynemer. A sickly young man, Guynemer was rejected by the French army more than once, but with the help of parental influence he managed to wangle his way into the Air Service, initially as a mechanic. A perfectionist, possessed of manic determination, he learned to fly, and was posted to MS 3, an Escardrille equipped with the Morane Parasol, on June 8, 1915. His first victory came on July 9, when his observer shot down an Aviatik in flames. His second was not to come for nearly six months. During this time, he practiced marksmanship, and paid great attention to the working of his machine-gun. By this time the unit had re-equipped with the Nieuport 11, and Guynemer's fighting career began in earnest, his fifth victory coming on February 5: an LVG down in flames. But over Verdun during March 1916, with his score at eight, he was wounded, and put out of the fight for a spell. At this time he was just one of a number of aces in the French Air Service; Jean Navarre, Charles Nungesser, Rene Dorme, Hertaux, Duellin and others were all making a name for themselves at about this time.

Returning to his unit in late May, his score began to mount. He usually fought in groups, as opposed to using formation tactics, but his style was reminiscent of Ball's, a rapid plunge and a quick burst from very close range, often less than ten meters. In September he exchanged his Nieuport for a Spad SVII; the Spad was less agile, but had a greater rate of climb, was much faster, and very tough. This suited Guynemer's style perfectly, his "taxi," as he called it, had the performance to force battle on slower opponents, and he developed a method of using a front quarter attack followed by a pull-up from underneath, which called for incredibly precise timing and judgement to be effective. Flying many times a day, he notched up his thirtieth victory on January 26, 1917, damaging an Albatros C type with his first ten shots, after which his gun jammed, then carrying out a series of dummy attacks which bluffed the German into landing in French-held territory. In this combat he was supremely aware of the power of suggestion, and got inside his opponent's mind very successfully.

Of course, not all combats were to end in victories; one in three was a good rate, even for the most skilled. In June of that year, Ernst Udet, the highest scoring surviving German ace of the conflict, encountered the Frenchman, and left this account:

> "At the same height, we go for each other, passing at a hair's breadth. We bank into a left turn. The other's aircraft shines light brown in the sun. Then begins the circling . . . Sometimes we pass so closely I can clearly recognize a narrow, pale face under the leather helmet. On the fuselage, between the wings, there is a word in black letters. As he passes me for the fifth time, so close that his prop-

wash shakes me back and forth, I can make it out: *"Vieux"* it says there ... That's Guynemer's sign. [Actually *Vieux Charles.*] Yes, only one man flies like this on our front ...

"I do a half loop in order to come down on him from above. He understands at once, and also starts a loop. I try a turn, and Guynemer follows me. Once out of the turn, he can get me in his sights for a moment. Metallic hail rattles through my right wing plane and rings out as it strikes the struts. I try anything I can, tightest banks, turns, sideslips, but with lightning speed he anticipates all my moves and reacts at once. Slowly I realize his superiority. His aircraft is better, he can do more than I, but I continue to fight."

Udet's gun had jammed, and it seems that Guynemer also had a stoppage at that time, as he broke off the combat and flew away. Udet firmly believed that Guynemer broke away when he realized that his opponent was helpless, but this does not accord with what we know of the Frenchman's character.

It is rare that protracted combats between high scorers occur, and this one lasted eight minutes in all. The interesting comment by Udet, who was a top aerobatic pilot in his own right is *"he anticipated all my moves!"*

Interestingly, we have another account of a similar one-versus-one encounter a few months later, by SE 5 pilot Cecil Lewis, of No. 56 Squadron.

"... I was badly worsted. Guynemer was all over me. In his hands the Spad was a marvel of flexibility. In the first minute I should have been shot down a dozen times. Nothing I could do would shift that grim-looking French scout off my tail. Guynemer sat there, at about thirty yards range, perfectly master of the situation."

A fast-moving airplane represents a lot of kinetic energy, and a lot of effort is needed to deflect it from its path. There is invariably a slight delay between control movement and the beginning of the maneuver. All that could account for this is that Guynemer was actually able to anticipate his opponent's moves. While he was unusual in this, he was not, of course, unique.

Guynemer fell on September 11, 1917, during the course

of a combat with a German two-seater. The circumstances are obscure, and he has no known grave. Like Ball, he had relied on attack, and to a degree disregarded defense. His final score was 53, and he had been brought down no less than eight times while achieving it. He was no tactical innovator, nor was he entirely at home in a formation. Like Ball, his value lay in his example, and the inspiration that it provided.

There can be little doubt that Georges Guynemer was caught up in the myth of the romance and chivalry of the air. His combat reports were brief and lacking in analysis, while his letters home were delightfully flippant, with such remarks as "the Boche in his excitement lost his wings, and descended on his airfield in a wingless coach; his ears must be humming." On the other hand, like Ball he was very technically minded, and was never happier than when up his elbows in grease. During the final year of his life, he liaised closely with the aircraft manufacturers, who adopted many of his suggestions.

As the war progressed, so the nature of air fighting developed and matured. In part this was due to technical progress. Stronger airframes and more powerful engines made for higher ceilings and greater top speeds. At the same time formation fighting, in ever increasing numbers, became the norm, although the lone wolf flyer, lurking high in the eye of the sun remained a factor until mid-1918. It became ever more important to recognize the capabilities of one's mount vis-a-vis that of the opposition. For example, the Sopwith Pup, with a wing loading of 4.82 lb/ft^2 and a power loading of 15.31 lb/hp, could outmatch the Albatros D III (wing loading 8.81 lb/ft^2 and power loading 12.18 lb/hp) at 16,000 ft., but its advantages slowly diminished with altitude, the German scout having a distinct edge at 10,000 ft. and below.

Controversy arose at this point as to whether the prime attributes of a fighter should be performance or maneuverability. It was never acrimonious, but often partisan, pilots tending to prefer the type of airplane which they flew. Major (later Marshal of the Royal Air Force) Sholto Douglas commanded No. 84 Squadron in France from September 1917 onward. No. 84 was equipped with the Se 5a, a fighter with an outstanding performance but moderate maneuverability. In a report written shortly after the end of hostilities, he summed up as follows:

> ". . . by virtue of your speed and climb, you yourself are always the attacker; which leads us to the conclusion that if your machines are superior in performance to those of the enemy, maneuverability is a very secondary consideration.
>
> "The reason why so many pilots insist on supreme maneuverability as an essential quality of a fighting machine is usually because they have only flown on active service fighting machines of inferior performance to those of the enemy. For instance the [Sopwith] Camel in 1918 was distinctly inferior to the German fighting machines. Camel pilots therefore often found their only salvation in the maneuverability of their machines. For they could not usually refuse combat when the enemy threatened to attack; they could not retire in order to return and fight under more advantageous conditions; by reason of the inferior speed of their machines they often had to submit to being attacked. They defended themselves—by maneuvering. Thus it is, I think, that some pilots have an exaggerated idea of the importance of maneuverability. To me it seems that it is performance that counts—performance is the all-important factor."

There are, of course, many who would disagree with this conclusion, pointing out that Camels destroyed more German aircraft in air combat than the SE 5. It should, however be said that Camel losses were higher, and that their exchange ratio was worse. It is also noticeable that out of the top four British Empire aces, three scored the majority of their victories while flying the SE 5a, while George McElroy, the tenth ranking ace, scored all 48 victories on the type.

What of the other major combatants? It is a matter of fact that the French preferred the highly wing loaded but speedy and strong Spad series to the more agile Nieuports, although the Germans seemed to have a preference the other way, many of their top scorers having a predilection for the Fokker Dr 1 Triplane, which by comparison with the later Albatros types was slow but very handy. It also had a very steep angle of climb, which enabled it to break off combat almost at will, or take an advantageous position above the ruck, ready to re-engage. The Richthofen brothers, Udet, Voss, Lowenhardt, von Schleich and many others all chose to operate the type. The final major type of German fighter to see service was the biplane Fokker D VII, which was both fast and agile, although not in the same league as the Dr 1 for maneuverability, and it had the disconcerting ability to hang on its prop at a steep angle while firing.

In the early days of air fighting, two entirely different sorts of successful pilots emerged, the rational and calculating thinker and innovator, typified by Boelcke, and the impetuous, not to say rash fighting pilot, of which Ball and Guynemer were prime examples. This trend continued, although it was modified a little by changing circumstances. The introduction of fighting formations by Boelcke's Jasta 2 in 1916 forced the British and French services to do the same in order to meet force with force; numbers with numbers. It was then up to the individual leader how he employed them, as a fighting team throughout the fight, or simply using the formation as a convenient method of getting large numbers to the fight efficiently, to get stuck in as individuals once engaged. A few pilots excelled in solo operations, stalking unsuspecting victims for the surprise attack, although they were few, and grew less as the war dragged on. Most commanders realized, as had Boelcke at an early stage, that the war was not going to end overnight, and that the philosophy to adopt was of doing the most damage for the least casualties.

Against this background, a new generation of aces emerged. Manfred von Richthofen, Ernst Udet and Werner Voss for Germany; Rene Fonck and Charles Nungesser for France, and Edward Mannock, Billy Bishop and James McCudden for the British Empire. What were the special qualities that set them apart from other men? What were they like as leaders? What results did they get and how did they get them? The qualities of a successful fighter pilot are easily stated. Good distance vision, alertness, marksmanship, determination, good aircraft handling, sound tactical sense, and that indefinable *je ne sais quoi* which warns them of danger, and tells them which way an encounter is likely to develop. In some men, all these qualities appear to be present from the outset. In others, some qualities are present from the start while others develop slowly.

Dealing with all of these factors in turn, it is safe to say that all the leading fighter aces had better than average distance vision, and also good depth perception. The difficult part was in teaching them what to look for. The average pilot saw nothing in his first few combats. Fairly typical was the experience of Lieutenant Cameron of No. 46 Squadron. On his first patrol on the evening of May 31, 1917, his flight of Pups ran into a bunch of Albatros D IIs over Roulers. A short, sharp fight followed, with no losses to either side. Back on the ground, the flight members discussed the engagement. Cameron, amazed, suddenly burst out: "What Huns? I never saw any. I thought you were all larking around to relieve the monotony, so I did a couple of loops, and let off fifty rounds at the moon!"

This experience was far from unique; there are many other similar accounts on record. As Vietnam "River Rat" Bill Lafever commented when shown this passage, "No contact, no visual, no clue!" Cameron lasted only a few days, but some pilots who went on to become very successful initially had the same problem. William MacLanachan, who survived the war with a tally of 21 victories, arrived at No. 40 Squadron not long after the legendary Mannock. He left this account of his first combat.

"A few evenings after my arrival, Captain Bath, leading us on a patrol between Lens and Lille, got into a scrap with some enemy fighters, and I had another disconcerting disillusionment about my capabilities as a fighter pilot. After seeing Bath wagging his wings to signify that enemy machines were near, the whole of the flight commenced to stunt and whirl about in the most disconcerting way. I did not see much of the fight . . . for except that the surrounding air seemed to be full of zooming, turning, and diving machines, I did not recognize more than one of these as German . . . To have been in a fight without having been able to discriminate between friend and enemy struck me as being the most dangerous form of stupidity. There had been seven German machines in the scrap and I had seen only one."

After a few weeks, MacLanachan began to train himself to see everything that was going on around him.

"I accustomed myself to watching everything that was going on in the line and on the German side. This practice in increasing my powers of observation stood me in good stead later on, but my principal object in consciously training myself was to avoid repeating the mistakes of the past. The quicker a pilot became accustomed to *"seeing"* everything that happened beside him, the greater was his efficiency and the better his chances of avoiding an untimely end."

Many very high scorers managed to pass this critical early stage at a time when the level of opposition was low, often flying observation machines rather than scouts. Others began their flying careers as observers. Manfred von Richthofen, Ernst Udet, Rene Fonck, Billy Bishop, Jimmy McCudden and Ira Jones all started in this way, which enabled them to build up their powers of observation slowly and at less risk than later flyers who were flung into the cauldron from the outset. Alertness was another facet allied to observation; the ability to react quickly and instinctively to a hazardous situation, and was learned in much the same way. Practice made perfect, although a prerequisite was to live long enough to gain the necessary practice. At the same time, many pilots seemed to develop a sixth sense warning them of danger. This occurs again and again in the memoirs and diaries of the period, and references to it are more common than might be thought. We will take a few at random; doubtless there should be many more, although some flyers such as Richthofen never mentioned it even though it seems that they possessed it in a high degree. Much depends on the character of the man. The Red Baron, like certain others, felt that he had a reputation to maintain. This comes over in his undoubted delight in medals and awards, his status as the ranking German ace, the odd worry that his younger brother Lothar would outdo him, and the often rather grudging and understated praise that he gave his subordinates. He was a killing machine, dedicated to being the best, and apparently lacking in humor. To ascribe even an iota of his success to some sixth sense rather than to his own undoubted skill and courage would have been to detract from his image as the greatest. He could never admit to being lucky, or anything else other than good. It may, of course, have been his armor against the cold wind of mortality; we shall never know. But often this sixth sense was admitted by others, or noticed by their comrades.

By May 1917, Ernst Udet was an experienced fighter pilot, having started by flying Eindeckers on the quiet Vosges sector. His six victories, out of his eventual tally of 62, had been amassed over a period of fourteen months. On May 25, 1917 he was leading a formation of five Albatros D IIIs of Jasta 15, commanded at that time by the 39-victory ace Heinrich Gontermann. The formation was V-shaped, with Puz Haenisch at one of the extremities. Udet recalled:

"I don't know if there is such a thing as a sixth sense. But suddenly I'm certain that we are in some sort of danger. I make a half turn—and in that instant I see, close to my side, not twenty meters off, Puz's aircraft enveloped in fire and smoke . . .

"Then his machine breaks up. The fuselage dives straight down like a fiery meteor, the broken wing planes trundling after it. I am stunned as I stare over the side after the wreckage. An aircraft moves into the range of my sight and tears westward about 500 meters below me. The cockades blink up at me like malicious eyes. At the same moment I have the feeling that it can only be Guynemer!"

It was not, of course, Guynemer, who brought down four aircraft on that day, all of them two-seaters. Nor was it Nungesser, who was stationed farther north, while Fonck was on leave, and it was unlikely to have been the ice-cool Rene Dorme, who failed to return on that day. It is only fair to say that Guynemer's reputation had given the German flyers a fixation about him, which led to Udet's faulty guess. On the other hand, the instinct that something was wrong was well-founded.

Billy Bishop, whose predatory instincts and marksmanship

Billy Bishop, whose predatory instincts and marksmanship made him the second-ranking British Empire ace. (RAF MUSEUM, HENDON)

made him the second-ranking British Empire ace, gave a perfunctory acknowledgement to a sixth sense as early in his hunting career as April 6, 1917, when he had been in France as a fighting pilot for less than four weeks. He wrote: "In these days I no longer had any misgivings as to whether a machine was friend or foe—I had learned to sense the enemy," a remark that smacks of Ball's "I smell them." Bishop's achievements are best put into perspective by comparison with a close contemporary. Arthur Gould Lee arrived at No. 46 Squadron (Sopwith Pups) toward the end of May of that year. In a letter home on September 7, he wrote, rather wonderingly " . . . he [Bishop] went on leave to Canada last month, complete with a VC, two DSOs and the MC—and he arrived in France only a couple of months before I did! He's shot down about 45 planes. How do people do it?"

Well might he ask. The Pup was contemporary and roughly the equivalent of Bishop's Nieuport, yet in spite of tremendous efforts, Gould Lee's victories could be counted on the fingers of one hand. When he left for home on January 1, 1918, Gould Lee could point to an honorable record of 222 hours over the lines, during the course of 118 patrols, including ground attack missions on camels in the later months, during which time he had had four aircraft shot from under him; notched up 56 combats and scored five confirmed victories, with a share in a further six. The main difference appears to lie in the fact that Gould Lee had not Bishop's penchant for lone wolf patrols, stalking and attacking superior numbers. For this he can hardly be blamed. He did the job that was required of him to the best of his ability, but he lacked that little extra something. Bishop, in a shorter period, flew more hours; carried out many more missions, had vastly more combats, some of which were absolutely hair-raising, and shot more accurately. What is more, he survived while doing so.

Sometimes the sixth sense is more rational. Charles Findlay flew the two-seater Bristol Fighter in 1918, with No. 88 Squadron. Less than a month after arriving in France, Findlay was assigned to reconnoiter a rail yard near Estaires at 12,000 ft. He recalled:

"Reaching the location and specified height, we began the operation: soon puffs of white smoke appeared in our vicinity. The observer was on his knees in the cockpit operating the camera, when the anti-aircraft fire suddenly ceased. I could see no immediate reason for this, and a sense of uneasiness took hold of me—I had the proverbial hunch,

"'Hang on,' I shouted to Gauntlett, my observer. Banking steeply to have a good look around, I was just in the nick of time. A solitary hostile triplane was climbing rapidly below us, its three plane edges faintly visible against the background of the earth. A few seconds more and we should have been raked from nose to tail without knowing what had hit us. With full power I dived, firing a burst into the small black fuselage; the enemy plane turned over on its back, and rolling over and over, crashed . . . Our first victory!"

Findlay ended the war with nine victories, one of whom was the German third ranking ace Erich Lowenhardt. In this case, there was a clue, the cessation of the anti-aircraft fire.

Another recorded case occurred on February 14, 1917, when Canadian-born Harold Hartney of No. 20 Squadron led a photographic sortie of two FE 2ds to Passchaendale.

"And again there came to me that peculiar feeling or sixth sense or whatever it is that has so often warned me of danger and saved my life. Jourdan [his observer] was busy with his camera, his head below decks, when that little voice said to me, 'Look for the burglar under the bed.' Instantly I craned my neck over the tail. There was Taylor [in the other FE], sailing along serenely two hundred feet behind us and a hundred feet higher. And right over him, like a burst of colored skyrockets, were seven brilliantly painted Albatrosses, single seaters, Richthofen's famous Flying Circus, diving right on us—*apparently from our side of the lines!*"

The resultant protracted dogfight went badly for the British, with both FEs shot down over their own territory and all crewmen injured or killed, although they were credited with two victories on their own account. But regardless of the eventual outcome, Hartney's instinct had saved them from being slaughtered like sitting ducks. Hartney was in fact convinced that he was downed by Richthofen himself, but this is unlikely. The master claimed two victories on this day, but both victims were BE 2cs.

William MacLanachan experienced a similar occurrence but in reverse. In mid-July 1917, he carried out a solo patrol during which he had an inconclusive encounter with four German aircraft. Returning, he had to let down through cloud.

"On diving through the cloud, to my complete amazement I found myself only a hundred yards behind a German Albatros. Pulling up to get a good sight on him, I held my fire until within about twenty yards. I was about to press the trigger when he looked around abruptly and dived away, leaving my machine spinning in his wash. My surprise at this was even greater than it had been on finding him. What made him look around at that particular moment when I was about to send him into eternity no one can ever know. Many pilots declared that there was a sixth sense that warned them of hostile thoughts near them."

The early part of this account is convincing, as it shows the narrator in a situation that was not to his credit, missing an easy chance, while the final sentence is revealing, showing that this form of SA was relatively common among experienced pilots. What is not known is whether it was there from the outset, enabling the pilots in question to survive and therefore become experienced, or whether it was a product of experience. It was probably both, some men having it from the start, while others developed it, although the latent ability had to be there. It is fairly easy to understand occurrences of this nature when a pilot was flying in a seemingly empty sky, but less so in the hurly-burly of a dogfight. Occasionally mid-air collisions happened, with friend or foe with frightening impartiality, but reading through accounts of the period, it seems amazing that they did not occur far more often than was in fact the case. In fact it seems that this same instinct operated in the dogfight, the following example also being supplied by MacLanachan from a fierce ccombat on August 22.

"In the most intense part of the fight my machine passed right across Mick's [Edward Mannock's] tail plane, only a few feet above him. I could see his eye was glued to his Aldis sight, aiming at an Albatros, but that inexplicable something that warned seasoned pilots of the proximity of another machine made him turn his head, only to realize in a fraction of a second that mine was a friendly machine."

Marksmanship was the next attribute. As the saying goes, good flying never killed anybody yet. To succeed, the budding fighter ace had to be aware of exactly what he could do with his weapons, and the answer was often surprisingly little. Most of the top scorers spent a tremendous amount of time sighting and aligning their guns correctly, and checking every round individually before loading to minimize gun jams, which in combat, were embarrassing, to say the least. Sights varied from the ring and bead to the telescopic, of which the Aldis was fairly typical. The ring and bead was better in the confused mêlée, as using the Aldis blotted out all vision of what was going on around except that through the viewfinder. McCudden records firing at and hitting opponents at distances of between three and four hundred yards using the telescopic sight, but this was only at non-maneuvering targets using no-deflection shots. In this he was exceptional, and the more usual approach was the "stick your nose in the enemy cockpit and you can't miss" method. Even then, it was not only possible to miss, but even more likely, to fail to inflict lethal damage. Keith Caldwell, of No. 60 and later commanding No. 74 Squadrons, was one of the most aggressive men ever to strap an airplane onto his back. Although he survived the war with a tally of seventeen confirmed victories, he was often seen hard on the tail of a German scout, firing for all he was worth at point-blank range without apparent effect, while Ball himself recorded missing from a mere five yards on one occasion. Marksmen who were consistently good at deflection shooting were very rare birds. Even Richthofen had problems in the early stages. He wrote: "At the time I did not have the conviction I have now that 'he must fall,' but rather, I was much more anxious to see if he would fall, and that is a significant difference. After the first or second or third miss, it occurs to you: 'So that's how you do it.' "

Mannock, later to become renowned for his deflection shooting had initial difficulties in hitting non-maneuvering targets. His first victory to come down on the British side of the lines had been a DFW on July 12, 1917. Having fired his gun many times without results, he had become convinced that he could not see a target correctly. Compelled to see the effect of his shooting, he rushed off to examine the DFW and the body of its pilot. It took this grisly experience to convince him that his fire was accurate, and give him confidence for the future. Only nine months later, one of his star pupils, Ira Jones, was having similar problems, and turned to Mannock for advice. Jones later recorded in his diary:

"I'm beginning to get a little depressed with my shooting. I have fired at sixteen Huns to date, and they are still alive . . . I've had a long talk with Mick about it. He thinks I am allowing too much for deflection. That is, I am aiming too much in front of the enemy. He has advised me to do a slight traverse; to sight about five yards in front of the engine, then to fire and, while firing, to bring the sight back as far as the pilot and then to push it forward again . . . This is what he says he did at first."

Within days, the first of Ira Jones' eventual forty victories had gone down.

Tracer was supposed to be an aid to aiming, and both sides used it extensively, but it could be very misleading. The burn time was variable in the extreme; sometimes it would extinguish itself quite quickly. If this happened before reaching the target, it would often appear that the bullets were vanishing into the enemy aircraft, whereas in fact they were falling short. In a fast-moving maneuvering combat, many pilots preferred to ignore their telescopic sight, and "hosepipe" tracer at their opponent. This was not very effective. The average pilot's judgement of range was abysmal, and often when he thought that he was firing from about 100 yards, the actual distance could be double, or even treble this. The high scorers tended to be good judges of distance. This, like many other things, could be learned.

Determination was an essential quality, although it should not be confused with rashness. It can be linked with courage, which in turn can be linked with the ability to overcome fear. Many pilots have been described as fearless, but this was hardly correct; they managed not to show it. Often this involved a tremendous personal battle for self-control. Typical instances were Ernst Udet, who encountered his first aerial opponent, a French Caudron, while flying an Eindecker in December 1915.

"He is now so close, I can make out the head of the observer. With his square goggles he looks like a giant malevolent insect coming toward me to kill. The moment has come when I must fire. But I can't. It is as though horror has frozen the blood in my veins, paralyzed my arms, and torn all thought from my brain with the swipe of a paw. I sit there, flying on, and continue to stare, as though mesmerized, at the Caudron now to my left."

The French observer commenced an accurate fire, and Udet, by now totally unnerved, disengaged and dived into the clouds.

The German pilot Ernst Udet whose eventual score was sixty-two victories. (POPPERFOTO)

Udet's experience was far from unique, although he recorded it more honestly than most. On the British side, Mannock and Jones suffered a severe reaction after their first combat which initially made them feel that they were unsuitable for flying duties, while there are several instances on record of pilots closing their eyes while performing their first loop, not even in combat. James McCudden went one better than this on November 9, 1916 when he attempted a loop in a DH 2, changed his mind halfway, and pulled some negative g which shot an ammunition drum into his propeller, wrecking it. Determination was in this case a little lacking, a fact that saved a German two-seater in January 1917, about which McCudden commented:

> "I honestly declare that I simply missed that Hun because I did not at that time possess that little extra determination that makes one get one's sight on a Hun and makes one's mind decide that one is going to get him or know the reason why."

Bishop also relates an example, this time from the hunter's point of view. "[The enemy] pilot now was gazing back over his shoulder and was too frightened to maneuver his machine. He had turned into a sort of human rabbit, and was concerned only with running for his life."

With Bishop on his tail, the end was swift and inevitable. Occurrences such as these were all too common. Under the threat of attack, many pilots either froze at the controls, or dived away in a straight line, giving their pursuer a no-deflection shot. Hence Boelcke's dictum that one should always fly to meet an attack, which he constantly pounded into the heads of his staffel members, firstly to get them to take some positive action and break the hypnotic state of inaction, and secondly in the expectation that training would reinforce determination and help to overcome fear.

The leading scorers were generally agreed that shooting ability and determination ranked above flying ability. Manfred von Richthofen explicitly stated: ". . . the decisive factor in victory is simply personal courage. One could be quite a splendid stunt flyer and still not be able to shoot down a single aircraft. In my opinion, stunting is all a waste of time . . . The spirit of attack, and consequently the taking of the offensive is the main point in the air . . ."

In this he was not entirely correct. If we take the corollary of an excellent marksman who is totally determined, but is a poor aircraft handler, he would still not get results, being unable for the most part to get his machine into a good shooting position except by sheer chance. Nor would he have the ability to reverse an unfavorable position. In short, he would be unlikely to last long. Many aces of both sides prided themselves on rarely getting shot up, among these being Heinrich Gontermann, Edward Mannock, James McCudden, and the Allied ace of aces Rene Fonck, who was rarely hit in combat.

Possibly the greatest aerobatic flyer of the war was Werner

James McCudden, one of the top-scoring British aces. (RAF MUSEUM, HENDON)

Voss, who was killed on September 23, 1917 during one of the epic fights of all time. Separated from the rest of his staffel, Voss first engaged two SE 5s of No. 60 Squadron, damaging both, before becoming embroiled with a further nine SE 5s of the craft No. 56 Squadron which included McCudden and five other pilots who were all to score more than twenty victories. Voss was shot shown by Rhys-Davids after a ten-minute combat, during which *all* the SEs were hit, two seriously damaged, and three written off. McCudden describes Voss, who had 48 victories at that time, as throwing his Fokker Triplane about in a very quick and uncertain manner, taking snapshots at all of them in turn. What Voss had succeeded in doing was to aggravate the amount of confusion already inherent in the fight by flying his machine in the most unpredictable manner possible. Much of the British pilots' SA was taken up with keeping out of each other's way, and Voss capitalized on this, being fairly unlucky not to add to his score while doing so. He could take shots of opportunity without having to bother overmuch about identification; anyone in his sights was certain to be an enemy, which was not the case for the British pilots. He could have disengaged at any time by climbing away; his fatal error was staying too long.

As formations grew ever larger, tactics played an increasingly important role. The formation leader now counted far more than the individual, leading his flight or staffel in the careful jockeying and sparring for position before launching an attack. There are only two candidates for the title of the greatest patrol leader of the war; Richthofen and Edward Mannock. Both ended as the ranking ace of their service; both were killed in action; and most significant of all, both produced a far higher than average proportion of high scorers from the men under their command. The Red Baron's Jasta 11 contained, among others, Lothar von Richthofen with forty victories, Kurt Wolff with 33, Karl Allmenroder with thirty, Karl Schaefer with thirty and Sebastian Festner with twelve, to say nothing of those who came under his influence with Jagdgeschwader 1. Mannock's scope was smaller; he commanded flights Nos. 40 and 74 Squadrons, but his only squadron command, No. 85, lasted less than four weeks. George McElroy with 48 victories; Ira Jones with forty, William Mac-

Edward Mannock, the Irishman who ended the war as the ranking British Empire ace. (RAF MUSEUM, HENDON)

Lanachan with 21, and "Dad" Roxburgh-Smith with seventeen, can be numbered among his pupils.

Their personalities could hardly have been more different. The calculating, ice-cold Prussian had nothing in common with the emotional Irishman. Richthofen regarded casualties as inevitable, whereas Mannock went to extraordinary lengths to avoid them, and in his two spells as a flight commander, lost only two members of a patrol led by him. The German was sparing with praise where the Irishman was lavish. On the ground, Richthofen emphasized the virtues of eating, sleeping, and not a drop of alcohol, whereas Mannock encouraged his comrades to release their tensions with riotous parties, although not to excess. Richthofen hoarded his victories jealously whereas Mannock not only gave away the occasional

Manfred von Richthofen, the "Red Baron," after his near miss on July 6, 1917, in hospital at Courtrai. (THE KEYSTONE COLLECTION)

kill to his flight to encourage them, but set up victories for the new boys to get them started. It was only natural for novices to be scared at first, and Mannock's method of overcoming this was to adopt a melodramatic bloodthirstiness, as though being shot down in flames was the funniest thing in the world. Richthofen stressed coordination while Mannock accentuated teamwork. Both got excellent results; there can be no doubt about that, and both were hero-worshipped by their followers. It was just that their methods were different.

Richthofen seems to have been content to follow Boelcke's rules, and apart from being a prime mover in the use of ever larger formations, culminating in the Jagdgeschwader made up of four Staffeln, contributed little to the advancement of air combat apart from his own sterling example. His philosophy was simple. "The fighter pilot should have an allotted area to cruise around in as it suits him, but when he sees an opponent, he must attack and shoot him down. Anything else is absurd." The one remarkable thing he did was to have his aircraft painted red all over. The reason for this is obscure. His brother Lothar stated that it was because he was frustrated by abortive attempts to find a paint scheme to make himself readily identifiable to other staffel members. Manfred himself described it purely as a whim. Neither explanation is entirely convincing. As leader, the elder Richthofen carried streamers for identification, while whims of this sort hardly equate with what we know of his character.

An all-red aircraft was not unique. Almost a year earlier Jean Navarre had used a red Nieuport, which had become widely known and feared by the German aviators on the Verdun front. Richthofen, aware that his reputation was spreading on the other side, and given his passion for trophies, and his habit of awarding himself a silver cup for each victory, may have wanted to stand out from his fellows, his red machine acting as a challenge, a throwing down of the gauntlet. It may also have been a psychological ploy to gain a moral ascendancy over his adversaries. But whatever the reason, the entire German fighter arm followed suit with bright paint schemes, which in a confused fight, made identification of friend or foe instantaneous.

Mannock was by contrast a meticulous planner. In the later stages of his career it was said of him, only half in jest, that by the time his patrol took off, they even knew what the Germans had had for breakfast. A pastmaster of ruses and deception, he often worried his own men as much as he worried the enemy. On July 7, 1918, he led No. 85 Squadron out on patrol, stepped up in three layers. Encountering ten Fokker D VIIs near Doulieu he played them for fifteen minutes to get them where he wanted them, before leading the lowest flight right beneath them. Half of the German force dived on him, only to be caught by the middle British flight, while the remainder, staying above to cover their comrades, were caught by the British top flight. Three Fokkers were shot down, while the hand of one British pilot was grazed.

Ira Jones recalled Mannock's leadership: "He was a forceful, eloquent speaker, with the gift of compelling attention.

After listening to him for a few minutes, the poorest, most inoffensive pilot was convinced that he could knock hell out of Richthofen or any other Hun."

It seems probable that Mannock had greater situational awareness than Richthofen, although a definitive judgment is not possible. The Red Baron has sometimes been unfairly criticized for picking on poor "helpless" two-seaters, as though air war was a sport rather than a deadly serious affair. In fact, 47 of his total of eighty victories were against two-seaters, but on two occasions he was downed by them. The first time was by a BE 2, which was generally regarded as a turkey by all sides. In March 1917, he held his fire a bit too long as he closed in for the kill, with the result that the BE 2 observer shot up his fuel tank and engine. Richthofen was lucky to get down without catching fire. On the following July 6 he was even luckier. Jasta 11 began a confused mêlée with the FE 2ds of No. 20 Squadron, and during the course of it, Richthofen made a head-on pass at one piloted by Captain Cunnell, who had eight victories to his credit at that time. The observer was Albert Woodbridge, who recalled seeing his fire splashing along the barrels of the Baron's Spandaus. One of his bullets caught the German flyer in the head before glancing off without penetrating the skull. Richthofen was unbelievably lucky to get down in one piece. In each case it seems that the Red Baron was taking a chance and allowing his opponent a clear return shot. On his final flight in April 1918, his awareness also seems to have deserted him. Chasing a Camel flown by "Wop" May, he appears to have got target fixation and failed to clear his tail, thereby allowing Roy Brown, in another Camel, to get a clear shot at him.

To return to the subject of "helpless" two-seaters, virtually every top scoring pilot got his share. On the other hand, many pilots of all nations considered a well-handled two-seater to be a match for a single-seater. James McCudden, who specialized in stalking high-flying reconnaissance aircraft, often commented on this, and occasionally was only too glad to let one go if it was well flown. Also one of the greatest fighters of the war was the Bristol, F2B. Very fast and strong, it was flown like a single seater, the gunner's sole function being to guard the tail. Andrew McKeever was the top scorer on the Brisfit, with thirty victories, and many others ran up respectable tallies. With pilot and gunner looking to fore and aft respectively, it was much more difficult to take by surprise than a single-seater.

When dealing with the exploits of the successful, air combat tends to sound notoriously deadeye. To correct this impression a few general details are given here.

Leonard Rochford flew Pups and Camels with No. 3 Naval Squadron, later No. 203 Squadron, RAF. He flew a total of 742 operational hours on the Western Front between February and September 1917, and January to October 1918. Officially credited with twelve confirmed victories, he records seven engagements in Pups, of which three were decisive, and 67 engagements in Camels, of which 25 were decisive. He recalled: "I was a slow starter, far from fearless, and anything but a good shot . . . it was a long time before I discovered that the best [ie, easiest] way to shoot down an enemy aircraft was to surprise him and get as close as possible before opening fire."

In February 1918, Rochford attended an air gunnery course at Berck sur Mer. Firing at a target floating in a pond, he scored seventeen hits from 200 rounds and fifteen hits from 120 rounds. He also fired 400 rounds at a drogue target towed by a BE 2c, scoring only seven inners and eighteen outers. This was about par for the course, and explains the poor results achieved by the majority of pilots. The average was rather less than one high achiever per unit. Ernst Udet commanded Jasta 4 between May and September 1918, during which time the unit gained a total of 71 victories. Of these, Udet accounted for no less than 39. This was not unusual. Carl Degelow commanded Jasta 40 from May 1918 until the Armistice, during which time he scored 26 victories out of the unit tally of 49. Some units had no outstanding scorers, and there were many of them, of all nationalities. Typical is the American 103rd Aero Pursuit Squadron, which between them flew 470 patrols, not to be confused with sorties, totalling more than 3,000 hours, between April 1, 1918 and the end of hostilities. They were credited with taking part in 327 combats, rather less than one every ten flying hours, in which they

Leonard Rochford, some of whose experiences and comments are recounted, is seen here at right with Sir Aubrey Ellwood, with whom he served in Naval 3. Behind them is a Sopwith Camel replica painted as Rochford's aircraft in 1918. (*HMS* HERON)

gained 45 confirmed victories plus two balloons for the loss of fourteen pilots, killed, missing or wounded. Their leading scorer was Paul Baer with eight, two of which were shared. He was shot down and taken prisoner near Laventie on May 22.

To summarize, the First World War was a time of basic learning, firstly how to use the new weapon, and then how best to apply it. As numbers increased, the confusion factor grew also, and the last year or so of the war was mainly spent in learning how to minimize confusion and keep the situation controllable. The privileged few demonstrated an instinctive understanding of this, while the better leaders tried to instill the basic principles into their followers. Of these, only Oswald Boelcke seems to have formalized principles into a basic code for air fighting, which in essence has stood the test of time.

Chapter 3

The Second World War

The exploits of the greater fighter aces in the first global conflict tend to obscure the fact that the only reason for the existence of fighter aircraft was to deny the enemy the benefits of aerial reconnaissance, artillery spotting, and the bombing of ground targets. Air combat is but a means to an end, it is not an end in itself. As Clausewitz stated, the aim in war is the destruction of the enemy. Air combat for its own sake would be a very expensive and inefficient way of achieving this.

During the twenty years that separated the First World War from the Second, tremendous technological advances were made. Engine power increased by a factor of four or five, while the weight per horsepower dropped dramatically. At the same time, supercharging ensured that maximum power was developed where it was wanted, in the air rather than at ground level. Reliability also improved greatly. Light metal structures replaced wood and linen, and innovations such as retractable undercarriages more than compensated for their extra weight. These advances benefited all airplanes, not only fighters. For the first time, aircraft could carry a worthwhile weight of bombs over a long distance, at speeds and altitudes that made interception by fighters a very chancy business. Fast high-flying reconnaissance machines could carry out their missions with little chance of interruption, while large aircraft could carry paratroops, or tow gliders. In a nutshell, the airplane as a weapon of war had become far more versatile and lethal.

From the mid-1920s, the bomber was increasingly seen as a war-winning weapon in its own right. Propagandists such as Lord Trenchard, and particularly the Italian General Douchet, saw the bomber as being able to destroy a nation's will to

As World War 2 progressed, a good view astern was to assume ever more importance, and the bubble canopy, as seen here on a Typhoon 1b, gained almost universal currency in the fighter community. (MoD)

continue hostilities by the systematic reduction of its munitions depots and of its manufacturing facilities, and by a lowering of the morale of the civilian population. The concept of total war had been born.

Against this threat, the fighter at first looked impotent. With little or no speed advantage over the bomber, it had to be in exactly the right place at exactly the right time at exactly the right height to even hope to effect an interception. The bomber had become the main threat, and fighter design was increasingly aimed to defeat it. This led directly to a new generation of fast, multi-gunned, monoplane fighters optimized for high speed, high altitude flight. Compared with their First World War predecessors, the fighter of 1940 was between three and four times more powerful, over twice as heavy, three times as fast, and could fly nearly twice as high. It carried up to four times the number of machine-guns, each of which had double the rate of fire of the earlier weapons; alternatively it carried cannon, the destructive power of which made the original weapon look like a popgun. Its rate of climb was about half as much again, a surprisingly small improvement accounted for by the fact that all else being equal, a biplane will always outclimb a monoplane.

The accent was on performance in order to catch the bombers and maneuverability suffered accordingly. There were two reasons for this: firstly, turning ability is a function of speed before anything else, and speeds had increased greatly; and secondly, turning ability is modified by wing loading, and wing loadings had increased by a factor of five or more. In consequence, the better First War scouts could turn through 180 degrees in four to five seconds with a radius of less than 200 feet; while their successors took seven to eight seconds using a radius nearly five times wider. The nature of the dogfight had altered; it was still confused, and just as dangerous for the participants, but the circles described by the antagonists were much larger and rather slower, even though the speeds were higher.

The quest for ever greater speed and altitude had yet another adverse effect. The pilot was now enclosed under a canopy which restricted his vision a little in some cases, and a lot in others, the Messerschmitt Bf 109E, with its heavy framed, girder-like "lid" being possibly the worst offender. While it was true that the low-winged monoplanes had no upper wing to blot out large sections of the sky above, in most early fighters the cockpit canopy was faired smoothly into the lines of the fuselage, thus restricting rearward vision. Rear view mirrors were widely used, and later became standard in the Second World War. A few first war pilots had used them; Albert Ball being the most notable, and their use was not unknown among the Germans, Richthofen actually commenting that he did not carry one. With the war well advanced, the bubble canopy, which afforded an excellent all-round view, was introduced. The Soviet Union went one better than this on their Yak series of fighters by using a bubble canopy, with a panel of toughened glass to protect the pilot from shots coming from astern while not affecting his rear visibility adversely.

Another area where visibility had deteriorated was directly forward. Two types of engines were in use, the inline, which was very long, and the radial, which tended to be on the fat

The Me 109E, showing the heavy framing to the canopy which ob-
scured the view from the cockpit. This particular aircraft was used for
comparative trials at Farnborough in June 1940 against the Spitfire, the
pilots being Wing Commander George Stainforth and Flight Lieutenant
Robert Stanford Tuck. The trials showed conclusively that the Spitfire
was the better fighter. At much the same time, the Germans evaluated
a captured Spitfire against the '109, and came to the opposite conclusion. The difference, of course, lay in the test regimes adopted; in practice there was little to choose between the two types, although the trials
did allow Stanford Tuck to "put himself into the enemy cockpit" during
later combat. (MoD)

side. The quest for speed meant that the pilot was set low in a
streamlined cockpit, and his view forward over the nose was
restricted. Some fighters were better than others in this respect; the inline-engined Macchi C 205 Veltro was very poor,
while the radial-engined Grumman Wildcat had the pilot
mounted relatively high, while the cowling sloped down at
about an eight degree angle, giving him what was arguably
the best view forward and down of any fighter of the period.

The restricted forward view was no big thing in flight,
although it could be embarrassing while taxiing on the
ground, but it was a distinct handicap if the pilot was trying to

Maneuverable, with a high rate of climb and fast acceleration, the Macchi C205 Veltro was excellent in the dogfight, but the forward view from the cockpit was simply appalling. Aimed deflection shooting was impossible, as at high angles off the target just disappeared beneath the long nose. (FLYPAST)

shoot at a maneuvering target. Aiming at a turning target involves allowing the correct amount of deflection, which means aiming in front of it. If the pilot has "saddled up" in pursuit, i.e., maneuvered his aircraft into the plane of motion of the target, which he has to do to get other than a fleeting snapshot, a large amount of deflection will put the target out of sight beneath his nose. The Hurricane, with its sloping cowling, was better than the almost straight-cowled Spitfire in this respect, even though both aircraft were fitted with the same Merlin engine.

The telescopic gunsight, which had demanded that the eye be glued to it while aiming, and the old ring and bead sight, were fast being replaced by the new reflector sight. In essence, this consisted of an illuminated circle with a central dot focused at infinity, reflected on a small perspex or glass square. Like its predecessors, it was inadequate for shooting at really large deflection angles, but as few pilots could hit a barn door even at small deflection angles, this was not too important. Its real advantage over the older types of sight was that if the pilot could see the illuminated ring and dot, his head must be in the correct position for aiming, while it left his peripheral vision free to pick up objects with relative motion, which might or might not be a threat.

With no radical improvements to the Mark 1 human eyeball, the visual envelope of the individual pilot remained exactly the same as in the earlier conflict, but the greater speeds shrank the time envelope considerably, the time between the initial sighting and reaching firing range becoming much shorter, typically about forty percent of that in the earlier conflict. Surprise was therefore much easier to attain, and this placed a premium on the ability to sight the enemy first and thereby gain the initiative. On the other hand, interception became more difficult, a fine judgement of the dynamics of the closing phase being necessary. Trials in the mid-1930s showed that fast bombers were notoriously hard to intercept. It was purely a matter of chance whether the bomber formation came within visual distance of the patrolling fighters, and even when they did, if they were at extreme range and not on a collision course, they might often slip past unobserved. The fighter needed some help to redress the balance.

This was forthcoming in electronic form. The advent of air-to-ground and air-to-air communications was to revolutionize air fighting. Until this time, only primitive means had been available; Very lights, rocking the aircraft in certain ways, and hand signals. Now pilots were actually able to talk to one another in the air and exchange information and warnings. A formation could break into its constituent parts, which could perform quite involved maneuvers under the direction of its leader. They could even operate out of visual contact with each other, above and below a cloud, for example, or from beyond normal visual distance. Previous air-to-ground communications had been even more primitive, consisting of strips of colored material laid out in prearranged patterns in a preset spot at best, while at worst, the fighters headed for the friendly anti-aircraft gunfire on the principle that there must be something hostile in the vicinity to justify it. Now the formation leader could receive instructions from the ground. All that was needed was a ground-based detection and reporting system to track intruders, and the fighters could be steered in the right direction.

The final link in the chain was forged when radar was developed as a workable system for detecting aircraft, enabling the defenders to see through clouds, and even track their quarry at night. It helped the fighters enormously to know precisely in which direction to concentrate their visual search, and a good controller on the ground became an essential part of the fighter team, directing them towards hostile formations, and warning them if they were getting into an adverse tactical situation. Throughout the course of the war, the combination of radar and ground control was never to become foolproof, but it did add greatly to the effectiveness of the fighters by increasing their SA. Once the fight was joined, its usefulness declined sharply, as like pilots in close combat, the confusion factor caused it to degrade. Still later counter-measures were introduced, and in the later stages of the war, a full-scale

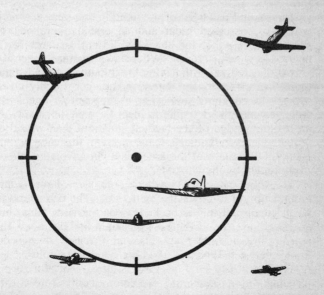

A standard World War 2 Fighter Command exercise for target range and deflection estimating. To be successful, a fighter pilot had to assess range, deflection angle, and target speed in a flash. Very few were much good at it.

electronic battle was waged in the background of the shooting war.

From this point, the air fighting can be split into four categories. The first took place in areas where there was no radar and virtually no ground reporting system, such as the Greek campaign in 1941, where air battles were fought on an encounter basis, often over the land battle areas. It is probably true to say that as in the Blitzkrieg on France in May 1940, more fighters were destroyed on the ground than in the air. A fighter spends far more of its time on the ground than in the air, and is far more vulnerable, being a sitting target. In the fast moving land warfare of World War 2, airfields were often over-run with their aircraft still on them. As the Poles, the French, the Russians, and finally the Germans discovered, the ultimate in air superiority is a tank in the middle of the runway.

The second category of air fighting was one in which the defenders possessed radar and an effective ground control system where either the attackers did not, or were forced to operate beyond its reach. Whereas in warfare generally the attacker is credited with having the initiative, this advantage is more than offset by the defender knowing roughly where he appears to be going and what he appears to intend doing, which enables the defender to react far more positively, based on his knowledge of the tactical situation, than would otherwise be the case. The classic examples of this category are the Battle of Britain, and the great daylight air battles over Germany fought by the USAAF.

The third category is where both sides have radar and ground control to cover the battle area. The defenders have a slight edge, and this is backed by anti-aircraft guns, but the attackers have the advantages of height and position. The offensive British fighter sweeps and Circuses over occupied France between 1941 and 1944 are typical examples.

The fourth and final category is the air war at night. Commencing with a situational awareness of almost nil at the outset, night fighting became an art before the end of the conflict. Target acquisition and weapons aiming had always to be visual. Unlike the day fighters, for which anywhere be-

Action replay. Nearly forty years on, ex-Luftwaffe members visit the RAF 11 Group operations room, from which most of the Battle of Britain fighting was controlled. In the center is the late Lord Willoughby de Broke, the Senior Controller during the summer of 1940, while to his left is Oberst Julius Neumann, an Me 109E pilot of Jagdgeschwader 27 at the time. Although far from perfect, the British radar and GCI organization played a crucial part in directing the defensive fighter battle. (MIDDLESEX COUNTY PRESS)

tween three and four miles, at any angle, and give or take a considerable amount of altitude was good enough in most cases, at night the controller had to place the fighter astern of the target, with preferably a little overtake, with little margin for error in altitude, and within about half a mile, to stand even a remote chance of bringing off a successful interception.

The next step was airborne radar carried in the night fighter, which extended its reach out to two or three miles ahead, and which eased the task of the ground controller considerably. With the airborne radar, the night fighter came of age; its effectiveness improved out of all recognition. The obvious next step was countermeasures to degrade radar, and night air combat became a seesaw between radar effectiveness and jamming. The story of night fighting can be regarded as a saga of the development of electronic SA aids, and is relevant inasmuch as it foreshadowed the trends of air warfare in the 1980s and onward. Interesting from our point of view is that just as a few fighter pilots in daylight instinctively knew what was going on around them, and what was likely to happen, so a few gifted black box operators managed to extract far more information from their equipment than the average.

In those early days, the radar information was presented in analogue form on either one or two screens, and interpretation of the displays was rather more of an art than a science. This was (and still is) the case with a few exceptional ground controllers, although today, the digital displays do most of the work.

Of all the major combatants in the Second World War, the Germans were the most advanced tactically, having derived the greatest benefit from their experiences in the Spanish Civil War between 1936 and 1939. Both Russia and Italy had taken

The Focke Wulf Fw 190 first appeared late in 1941, and out-performed the current mark of Spitfire so well at first that a raid was planned to capture an example and test fly it to find out if it had any weak points. The raid was called off when an Fw 190 got lost and landed on a British airfield. Rarely had knowing the strengths and weaknesses of an adversary seemed so important. (FLYPAST)

part in this conflict, but without learning a great deal. In the Far East, Japan fought a prolonged war against China, and also clashed briefly and bitterly with the Soviet Union. Without radar, and mostly without radio, the fighting in these conflicts was similar in nature to that of the First World War, arising from encounters between patrolling or escorting fighters. The Germans, in the shape of the Kondor Legion, had relearned the virtues of the pair as the minimum fighting unit, with the leader attacking and his wingman protecting his tail, which had been widely used in the earlier conflict, and also the *schwarme* formation of two pairs flying in slightly staggered abreast, which allowed good mutual cross-cover to be given to the vulnerable rear quadrant. With air-to-air radio communications, it was found that the situational awareness of the *schwarme* was many times better than the sum of its individual pilots' SA. All other nations stayed with the three-aircraft Vic formation as the basic unit, to their eventual detriment. This was the situation when the Second World War broke out.

Having overwhelmed the Polish Air Force with both quality and quantity, the Luftwaffe spearheaded the successful invasion of Denmark and Norway, then turned their attention to France. The French fighter pilots, in their generally outclassed machines, Morane MS 406s, Bloch 151s, Curtiss Hawk 75s and a handful of Dewoitine D 520s, put up a tremendous fight, ably assisted by several Hurricane squadrons of the Royal Air Force, but were disadvantaged by the lack of an effective early warning and reporting system. Had the ground forces held fast, this might not have been too bad, but the overall situation deteriorated, and the air defenses virtually fell to pieces, but not before they had shown their fighting quality. The French top scorers were all Hawk 75 pilots of Groupe de Chasse 1/5; Edmond la Meslée claiming fifteen confirmed victories, followed by Michel Dorance and Camille Plubeau, each with fourteen. The RAF top scorer was New Zealander Edgar James Kain with a total of seventeen.

The pre-war Royal Air Force had concentrated on defense against massed bomber attacks to the exclusion of almost all else. Now they were to be confronted with the prospect of escorted bomber attacks from the other side of the English Channel. All practice fighter versus fighter combat had been one versus one, with aircraft of the same unit, unlike the Luftwaffe who, profiting from their Spanish experience, had instituted formation fighting practice, accepting the collision risk by so doing. On the other hand, the British had a comprehensive radar detection and reporting system which was to go a considerable way to redressing the balance. Tactically, they had a long way to go, with the only school being the hard one of combat.

In the early days of the Battle of Britain, most squadron commanders stuck to the outdated stereotyped attacks that had been instituted to deal with bomber formations, but a few instinctively felt that this was wrong. One of the earliest examples was Robert Stanford Tuck, who on his very first mission, over Dunkirk on May 23, noted that when No. 92 Squadron flew through a patch of turbulent air, the formation lost cohesion for a few seconds. This left him feeling uneasy; the tight "air show" formation took too much concentration for keeping station at the expense of watching the sky. On a second sweep that day, the squadron CO was lost, and Stanford Tuck was given temporary command. The very next morning, on his first mission as leader, he opened the formation up until the Spitfires were about 200 feet apart. This was not as much as the Germans used; the formalized *schwarme* officially had 600 feet between aircraft, although frequently the actual spacing was barely half this. His next innovation came very swiftly; scrapping the three aircraft section and replacing it with the pair, operating as leader/wingman. This was possibly the first time that this was done in RAF Fighter Command, although it had often been used in 1917-18.

Stanford Tuck was a brilliant aerobatic pilot, and very unusually, a long distance marksman, frequently firing (and hitting) from distances of between 2,000 and 2,500 feet. In the early days of the eight-gun fighters, the guns were harmonized to give a pattern at 1,350 feet, and this was later amended to give harmonization on a point at 750 feet, while individuals, for example James Lacey (29 victories) had the guns of his Hurricane point harmonized at 450 feet. Most high

Robert Stanford Tuck, the brilliant aerobatic pilot and marksman, who was shot down and taken prisoner with a score of twenty-nine victories. (RAF MUSEUM, HENDON)

scorers, Lacey among them, and certainly the majority of German aces, adopted the "stick your nose in the enemy cockpit" approach, to make sure that their shots counted. Marksmen of the Stanford Tuck breed were very rare, and only the Canadian George Beurling, the Malta top scorer, springs to mind as being in this category.

As a fighter leader, Stanford Tuck was in the top rank. He was shortly "talent spotted" and sent to command No. 257 Squadron, which was demoralized after a bad beating. That he succeeded is attested by George Barclay of No. 249 Squadron, based at North Weald, who noted in his diary on October 9, 1940, "257 Squadron have arrived to take the place of 25 Squadron . . . [they] strike me as being very proud of them-

A well known picture of Spitfire is of No. 92 Squadron RAF. Leading the formation in the nearest aircraft is future 29 victory ace Robert Stanford Tuck, with Charles Kingcombe alongside. (MoD)

selves, and are quite determined that they are the only squadron in the RAF."

Stanford Tuck's SA was also well above average, although renowned as he was for an incredible series of escapes, this might not always seem the case. His biographer, Larry Forrester, says of him: "Sometimes it was hard to see how he had reached certain conclusions—how he could have known that a situation was going to develop the way it did. There is some sixth sense that a man acquires when he has peered often enough out of a perspex capsule into a hostile sky—hunches that come to him, sudden and compelling, enabling him to read signs that others don't even see. Such a man can extract more from a faint tangle of condensation trails, or a distant flitting dot, than he has any reason or right to do."

On the other hand, he often led his squadron or wing into battle from an adverse position when the tactical situation demanded it. For example to strike at the bombers before they had reached their targets often called for him to engage from below on the climb ignoring the escorting Messerschmitts as far as possible. Unusually, his sixth sense also worked for him on the ground as well as in the air. One evening in October, he felt a compulsion to leave a pub early; irrationally, he just *had* to go. Shortly afterwards it was bombed, and several pilots still there were killed or injured. Like many other high scorers, he was shot down by ground fire and taken prisoner, with his tally at 29.

One of the great British fighter leaders, and the one who probably did the most to get the tactics of battle right, was the South African Adolph (Sailor) Malan. A quiet, abstemious disciplinarian, Malan was unhappy from the outset with the three-aircraft section, and with his elevation to the command of No. 74 Squadron, switched to pairs flying in line astern, with two pairs in line astern making up a section. When the whole squadron flew together, the three trail sections formed up as a vic. Although not as good as the German *schwarme*, it was a great advance on what had gone before. He also advocated that squadrons gained height away from the enemy, only engaging when they had the advantage. But his main claim to fame lay in his Ten Rules for Air Fighting, which he had been

One of the great British fighter leaders, Adolph "Sailor" Malan, the brilliant South African tactician. (RAF MUSEUM, HENDON)

preaching for many months before formalizing them in August 1941 (rather than September 1940, as is so often stated). They are:

1) Wait until you see the whites of his eyes. Fire short bursts of one or two seconds, and only when your sights are definitely "ON."
2) Whilst shooting, think of nothing else, brace the whole of your body, have both hands on the stick, concentrate on your ring sight.

3) Always keep a sharp lookout. "Keep your finger out!"
4) Height gives *You* the initiative.
5) Always turn and face the attack.
6) Make your decisions promptly. It is better to act quickly even though your tactics are not the best.
7) Never fly straight and level for more than thirty seconds in the combat area.
8) When diving to attack, always leave a proportion of your formation above to act as top guard.
9) INITIATIVE, AGGRESSION, AIR DISCIPLINE, and TEAMWORK are words that MEAN something in air fighting.
10) Go in quickly—Punch hard—Get out!

The above may seem fairly basic, and in truth it does not differ much from Boelcke's rules of a quarter of a century earlier. The fact is, however, that air combat is a very complex subject, and the average pilot, as apart from the few gifted and instinctive air fighters, finds it very difficult to grasp. It is all fairly simple while the enemy is sailing along straight and level, but the instant he starts to maneuver, it becomes extremely difficult. The object of the exercise, as with all sets of instructions, is to give the learner, whose SA level is nil in most cases, a set of guidelines to enable him to survive long enough to commence the learning process. It is also essential to make him feel that he is doing something aggressive, and not just flapping about learning to survive, as this would do nothing for his self-confidence, and make him easy game for an experienced opponent.

Rules 1 and 2 are concerned solely with shooting. If a novice were to find himself in good position by some accident, and it has often happened, it would be a tragedy if he were to throw away the chance. Rule 3 is basically survival, as is, indirectly, rule 4. Rule 5 is pure Boelcke and for exactly the same reasons, while rule 6 again reverts to survival, saying in effect, "don't hang around and give an opponent an easy shot; also, don't be indecisive." Rule 7 is again pure survival. Provided that no one has managed to attain a good attacking position unobserved, thirty seconds is about how long it will take an opponent to do so. Rules 8 and 9 reflect the degree to which air combat had become a matter of teamwork and mutual support. The final rule was possibly the most important of all; to keep the situation controllable. A surprise attack followed by repositioning for a further surprise attack was liable to yield better results than a surprise attack followed by a dogfight, although the latter was often unavoidable.

Unfortunately, fighter leaders of the caliber of Malan and Stanford Tuck were in the minority during those hectic days of 1940. Johnnie Johnson, who was to end the war as the ranking British ace with 38 victories, attended an Operational

Johnnie Johnson, who was to end the war as the ranking British ace with thirty-eight victories. (RAF MUSEUM, HENDON)

Conversion Unit at Hawarden early in August of that year. He was later to comment:

> ". . . Although the instructors were good fellows they were few and we were many, and they seemed content to teach us to fly the Spitfire but not to fight it. We searched desperately for someone to tell us what to do and what not to do, because this, we fully realized, would shortly mean the difference between life and death. We knew we were about to face a period of great personal danger, and that if we survived our first few fights we would be of some value to our squadrons. But our problem was how to get through half a dozen fights? We wanted a man of the caliber of Boelcke or Mölders or Mannock or Malan to explain the unknown and to clear our confused and apprehensive minds; but on this occasion the right senior officer was not present."

This was not a problem for the Luftwaffe, who had ironed out their tactics in the Spanish Civil War, and honed them in the skies of Poland and France. Under such leaders as Theo Osterkamp, who had gained 32 victories in World War 1, and Werner Mölders (fourteen in Spain), and having had the benefit of more realistic training than the RAF, the tyro pilots knew exactly what to do and how to go about it. Mölders in particular was a quiet, thinking leader, obsessed with getting the tactics correct. He once remarked that if Adolph Galland (104 victories) wanted to be the new Richthofen of the Luftwaffe, he was content to be its Boelcke. On the other hand, one cannot help but feel that the RAF was unlucky to be troubled with Mölders, who notched up 115 victories on all fronts, for as long as it was. He was shot down twice; the first time by a French Morane, after which he was taken prisoner but repatriated at the Armistice, while on the second occasion, which occurred on July 28, he led two Gruppen of Jagdgeschwader 51 in an attack on twelve Spitfires of No. 74 Squadron. Turning in behind the British leader, who happened to be Sailor Malan, he found himself outmaneuvered and was raked from end to end by machine-gun fire, barely managing to nurse his

Werner Mölders, whose experience with the Luftwaffe in the Spanish Civil war made him a formidable adversary. (RAF MUSEUM, HENDON)

damaged Bf 109 back for a crash landing at Wissant. He was wounded in this action.

The above incident may have been partly responsible for the Luftwaffe's adoption of hit and run tactics against the more maneuverable English fighters. Mölders and Galland concluded in one of their many discussions that there was no point in trying to dogfight the Spitfire, as this was to fight on their opponent's terms. In support of this is the letter home written by a young pilot in Mölders' Geschwader on August 17:

> "Often the Spitfires give beautiful displays of aerobatics. Recently I had to watch in admiration as one of them played a game with thirty Messerschmitts, without itself ever getting into danger; but such individuals are few."

Unfortunately it has been impossible to discover the identity of the British flyer. For a single pilot to engage a whole Gruppe of Messerschmitts, which were led by Mölders himself, without ever looking like getting into trouble, was no mean feat, and his SA must have been remarkable. On the other hand, the old truism that good flying "never killed anyone yet" also seems to apply.

Mölders seems to have been the sort of inspirational fighter leader who was selfless with his own personal score and, like Mannock some 22 years earlier, gave away the occasional victory to encourage a young pilot. One of his main concerns was to ensure that a young pilot obtained his first kill without too much shock. Killing while avoiding being killed can be a traumatic experience, and too horrendous a time occasionally could make a pilot operationally useless. Perhaps his one major error was to approve the substitution of the two 20 mm MGFF cannon in the Bf 109E for the single (although faster-firing) 15 mm MG 151 cannon in the Bf 109F-2. Mölders was an outstanding marksman, and in his hands this reduced armament was sufficient against enemy fighters, but it was a retrograde step for those of lesser ability. Adolf Galland, and others of the "stick your nose in the enemy cockpit" club, opposed this measure, and with hindsight we can see they were right.

The same attitude but in reverse was evinced by the legendary Douglas Bader, who was arguably the most inspirational fighter leader of all. Headstrong and opinionated, Bader argued for the retention of the eight machine-gun armament against either two or four 20 mm Hispano cannon. He also was wrong in this instance, and cannon became the standard RAF fighter armament, although the Americans were to stay with the hard hitting .50-inch caliber machine-gun to the end of the war almost without exception.

Bader was quick to see from the outset that the standard Fighter Command Attacks were a waste of time; he was less quick to junk the unwieldy three-aircraft section. He did, however, introduce the "finger four" fighter formation, although this was not until 1941. The finger four became standard throughout both the British and American services before

One of the most inspired fighter leaders of all time, Douglas Bader is seen here standing on the wing of his Hurricane in October 1940. (POPPERFOTO)

the end of the war, although Malan's fours in line astern lingered well into 1943 with some units. He also introduced the "big wing" concept in the summer of 1940, but this was not very successful. While three, and later five squadrons of fighters could be got off the ground quite quickly, reaching altitude and getting them into the correct position was a time-consuming process which did not make for effective interceptions. Even with the benefit of radar and close ground control, the average fighter squadron operating alone only made contact with the incoming German armadas on about one in every three occasions. The record of the big wing was rather worse.

Bader really came into his element as the Tangmere Wing Leader, operating defensively over France in 1941. His teamwork with Group Captain Woodhall, the ground controller, was really exceptional. Receiving the broad picture from the ground controller, he handled his three fighter squadrons with remarkable dexterity once in action, seemingly able to foresee the critical points of the coming engagement. He was also able to keep track of events around him to a remarkable degree, and at debriefing afterward was able to build up the broad picture of events better than anyone else.

His real claim to fame lies in the example that he set to others. Quite apart from the fact that almost every fighter pilot in the RAF said to themselves at one time or another, "if a chap with no legs can do it, then so can I," his total refusal to be impressed with anything, be it a lack of legs, a hundred German fighters lurking in the sun, an irate Air Marshal, or the Kommandant of Colditz, lifted and inspired those with whom he flew and fought. As Stanford Tuck said of him, after a typical piece of defiance in a prisoner of war camp: "in that moment, he was the leader of us all." *Enfant terrible,* fighter ace, international class sportsman, inveterate rule-breaker and incorrigible escaper, he spread inspiration and exasperation wherever he went. Smoking his pipe in the cockpit one moment, and adamant teetotaller, he is impossible to classify.

When one examines the records of the fighter pilots of the First World War, one finds a remarkable similarity of performance. The ranking aces of the major powers have all roughly the same scores, while proportionately the higher scorers do not vary by much although, as has been noted, the Germans come out rather the better. This is not at all true of the second conflict. The top scoring German and Japanese pilots easily outperformed their Allied opposite numbers; in the case of the Germans, often by incredible margins. The Allied top scorers were Pat Pattale, with between forty and fifty (the records are incomplete); Johnnie Johnson with 38, and American Richard Bong with forty. One of two conclusions can be drawn. Either the Germans, and to a lesser degree the Japanese, are better natural fighter pilots than those of the Anglo-Saxon nations, or there are other forces at work. When one considers that the German top scorer was Erich Hartmann, with the amazing total of 352, followed by Gerd Barkhorn with 301, and that both survived the war, the difference is glaringly apparent. The Japanese did less well, Hiroyoshi Nishizawa leading the field with 87, while the ranking surviving ace was Saburo Sakai, with a total of 61. There were many other German high scorers. A further thirteen pilots topped the 200 mark, while twenty more notched up 150 or over. Of these, roughly half survived the war.

It is easy to establish that none of these men flew fighters that completely outclassed those of the opposition for all of their fighting careers; generally this was the case for relatively short spells, and most of the time they were opposed by fighters of equal and sometimes greater capabilities. It is equally ridiculous to say that these results were the classic example of overclaiming. While none of their records can be absolutely verified, a high proportion of their claims check out. If they did not, the vast amount of painstaking research that has been carried out over the intervening years would have revealed the fact by now. It seems that we must look for other factors to account for this discrepancy.

In a previous chapter we established that the victory per hundred sorties ratio tended to reduce as the number of participants increased. It was also fairly clear that the more adverse the sortie ratio became, the more dangerous the outnumbered force became. Equally obvious was the fact that surprise was the dominant factor in air combat, and that something around eighty percent of all aircraft shot down were taken by surprise, the remaining twenty percent being the result of dog-

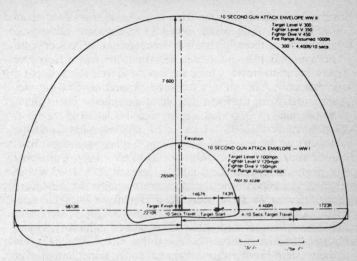

Performance outstripped maneuverability basically because it enlarged the envelope from inside which a fighter could make a gun attack within ten seconds, which in turn greatly enhanced the value of the surprise bounce. Here we have the ten second attack envelope at typical World War 2 speeds superimposed on the same attack envelope at typical World War 1 speeds. The difference is quite remarkable, even allowing for the fact that firing ranges have increased from an average 450 ft. in the First World War to 1,000 ft. in the Second.

fights, during the ensuing maneuver phase. To a degree, it is the old argument about winning all the battles but losing the war. Now the fact is that both the Germans and the Japanese lost the war, but produced the highest scoring fighter pilots. Let us look into this a bit more closely.

Not every operational sortie results in a combat. Even when a combat does take place, it does not even necessarily involve firing one's guns at the enemy. It all boils down to a question of opportunities. Generally speaking, both the side that is on the defensive, and the side that is outnumbered, will get more opportunities to score. A brief glance at the list of German aces shows that almost without exception, the highest scorers achieved the majority, if not all their kills on the Eastern Front, flying against the Russians. Hartmann scored all of his 352 there, while of the other 33 flyers who notched up totals of 150 or more, only Hans-Joachim Marseille scored all of his eventual 158 victories in the West, the vast majority of these coming in North Africa against the Desert Air Force. Of the rest, only five got a substantial proportion of their victories in the West, the most notable of these being Heinz Baer, of whose total of 220 victories 96 were achieved in the East, about forty over North Africa, a handful over Italy, and the remainder on the tough Western Front. Flying against the British and Americans in the West seems to have been a different ball game altogether. Discounting Marseille, 151 of whose victories came in Africa, the top scorers against the West were Heinz Baer as we have seen, Kurt Buehligen with 112 victories, Adolph Galland with 104, and Joachim Muncheberg and Werner Schroer with 102 each with total tallies of 135 and 114 respectively. It should be noted that of these, quite a few of the western Front victories were actually gained either over Malta or the Western Desert. Finally we have Egon Mayer with 102, all scored in Western Europe, and Josef Priller with 101. From this, it seems that victories were easier to come by against the Russians than against the British and Americans.

There were many reasons why this was the case. In the first eighteen months or so of the war, most Soviet fighters were outclassed by the Bf 109 by quite a margin. The Soviet pilots were ill-prepared and barely trained, and were shot down in droves. Few of them had any idea tactically, while their high command was also sadly lacking, sending out attack aircraft and bombers in small packets without fighter cover. Soviet aviation was so attuned to supporting the ground forces that even when fighters were present, they were invariably below the German fighters, where they were easily bounced from above. They had no radar, and their detection, tracking and ground control system was rudimentary where it existed at all. They had but two advantages, which in the long run were to prove decisive: a vast pool of manpower and tremendous potential industrial strength. Only when these two factors could be effectively mobilized could the Soviet Union redress the balance. Finally, Germany had limited manpower and industrial resources, which were stretched to and finally beyond breaking point as the Western powers stepped up their air assault, at first over France and the Low Countries, and finally over the Reich itself. Once the Soviet Union had survived the initial onslaught, albeit with horrendous losses, her armed forces, and the air arm was not the least of these, grew to be an unstoppable juggernaut.

In the early days of the campaign against Russia, the German pilots often encountered Soviet pilots in the air who had little or no idea how to defend themselves, and who were easy pickings. Later in the war, with Soviet training schools and industrial output on the upsurge, a whole flood of raw pilots was reaching the front, albeit in better aircraft than had previously been the case. By this time, the needs of other theaters—Malta, the Desert, Italy, the defense of the homeland—often caused forces to be withdrawn from the East, with the result that the German fighter forces remaining were very heavily outnumbered. Stretched to the limit, the German fighter pilot in the East had more targets than he could reasonably handle.

Gerd Barkhorn and Gunther Rall, the second and third ranking German aces, with 301 and 275 victories respectively, achieved much fame in the early days, both being reputed to have shot down a hundred Russian aircraft in the first few weeks of the invasion of the Soviet Union. Both had flown extensively in the battle of Britain, with little success, Barkhorn not scoring and Rall getting just three. In all, Barkhorn flew no less than 1,104 operational sorties for his 301 victims, but when transferred back to the West, again achieved nothing. Rall scored at a rather faster rate, but flew less sorties. Another ace who was very successful in the early days of the Russian campaign was Hermann Graf, who after scoring his first victory in August 1941, passed the 200 mark early in October 1942. His eventual total was 211.

By contrast, the progress of the man who was to surpass them all seems positively pedestrian. Erich Hartmann arrived on the Eastern Front straight from training school late in 1942, just as the Soviet Air Force was beginning to get its act together. After some eight months, his score had climbed to a

Gunther Rall, the third ranking German ace with 275 victories to his credit. (HUBERT ZEMKE)

modest twenty. Then in July and August of 1943 he suddenly, like Richthofen before him, discovered how it was done, sending down no less than 78 Russian aircraft over the two months, including seven in one day on July 7, in the course of three encounters. From this moment he never looked back. His 352 victories were scored in the enormous total of 1,425 sorties, during which the enemy was encountered on 800 occasions.

Hartmann was a cautious flyer, always seeking out the most advantageous position from which to attack. He was also a member of the "stick your nose in the enemy cockpit" school. On many occasions he scored multiple victories, but was more often content to get one and then break off the action, also like Richthofen, who once accused his younger brother Lothar of being a shooter rather than a hunter because he was never satisfied with just one scalp per fight. The remarkable thing is how his nerves stood the strain of continuous flying and fighting. In all he was shot down eighteen times, being taken prisoner once but escaping. It should also be remembered that not all Soviet fighter pilots were turkeys. Their top scorer during the conflict was Ivan Kozhedub with 62 victories, closely followed by Alexandr Pokryshkin with 59, Grigorii Rechkalov with 58 and Nikolai Gulaev with 57; three other pilots topped the fifty mark, a further eight scored forty or more and 35 reached or passed thirty. There are also persistent rumors that one pilot attained a score of about eighty victories, but was purged as being politically unreliable.

Hartmann's operational philosophy could be encapsulated in just four words—See, Decide, Attack, Break or "coffee break." Enlarged a little, the situation had to be carefully but quickly assessed and the decision taken whether or not to attack. The attack had to be carried out swiftly and cleanly, followed by a break to re-assess the situation. If the circumstances for attack were not favorable, then the answer was a "coffee break," to go and look for someone who was not going to play so rough. Although he was often downed himself, Hartmann was proud of the fact that he never lost a wingman. As he used to tell young pilots joining his unit: "There are some things that are more important in the overall picture than just scoring a kill. The Russian Air Force is numerically large and getting larger all the time. If you score a kill and lose your wingman, you have lost the battle."

Little convincing material is available from the Soviet side, but the Russian fighter pilots did have a few tricks to make life difficult for the German flyers. Often banded into elite units, the Guards Regiments, they quickly adopted the pair as the basic formation, the spear and the shield, as Colonel Dubovitskiy dubbed them in an article in the late 1970s. They also tended to fly everywhere at full throttle; not on emergency power, which would have blown up their engines in short order, but maximum normal power. This increased their cruising speed which became flat out for all practical purposes, which had the effect of making the surprise bounce more difficult for the German pilots to achieve. Not only did it become more difficult to judge, but the extra speed made it more difficult to get into position, while the whole process took longer, giving the Russians more time to see the attack coming in and maneuver to defeat it. They also tended to fly in large, undisciplined-looking formations, swirling around the sky like a flock of starlings. This also made them difficult to surprise, as while the formation was going in one direction, its component sections were at all different heights and were rarely all pointing the same way at one time. This may or may not have been deliberate, but its effect was to make it very difficult for a would-be attacker to select a victim while keeping his escape route clear.

By comparison with the Luftwaffe fighter pilots, those of other nations flew far fewer sorties, very few reaching the 500 mark. Their opportunities were also generally rather less, only the Japanese operating in the target-rich environment provided by United States air power in the Pacific, and even there the intensity of operations was less. Kozhedub's 62 victories were gained in the course of 330 sorties with 120 combats, while Pokryshkin's score of 59 took 360 sorties with 156 combats. For the Allies, Johnnie Johnson flew 515 sorties for his 38 victories, while Frenchman Pierre Clostermann scored 33 in 420 sorties. The opportunities simply were not there. Johnson's Spitfire was only hit once in air combat, which is a remarkable record, and then only when, separated from his unit and trying to rejoin, he pulled in front of six Bf 109s in the belief that they were his Spitfires and told them to reform on him! They did, almost fatally.

Misidentification was not all that uncommon, even with very experienced pilots. One of the oddest occurrences was the story of the non-existent Heinkel He 113, which had its roots in a prewar German propaganda exercise. This fighter was frequently reported as being seen during the battle of Britain. Sailor Malan commented to First World War ace Ira Jones that the He 113 was often mistaken for a Spitfire, which it resembled although it had a fatter fuselage. George Barclay of No. 249 Squadron often referred to them in his diary, although a couple of clues emerge as follows: ". . . one has to be extremely careful as the German fighters use every device to try to disguise the Me 109 and He 113 as Hurricanes and Spitfires respectively" (September 23, 1940); and "We saw some He 113s above us—everyone except Millington and I thought they were Spitfires . . ." (October 10, 1940).

In fact, the Germans did everything possible to make sure that there was no chance of mistaken identity, especially in the confusion of close combat, which is why they adopted the custom of painting the noses of their fighters yellow, and not, as is so often stated, the mark of an elite unit. But as someone who once misidentified an F-15 as an F-4 (it was at an odd angle), the author feels that no one should be too critical of these things.

Malan, Stanford Tuck and others had run up respectable scores fighting at odds against the Luftwaffe, but the leading German pilots had done rather better. This was due to the nature of the conflict; whereas the Spitfires and Hurricanes made the bombers their priority, the Messerschmitts—usually with an altitude advantage—had no such restriction. Also, German teamwork tended to give their formation leaders more and better opportunities than the men they led. But when in the following years the scenario shifted to Northern France, the British wing leaders came to the fore. Of these, Brendan Finucane, the Kenley wing leader, was possessed of outstanding SA.

Finucane was blessed not only with perfect vision, but also with incredible powers of concentration. It was once said of him that while leading his wing he could keep track of four different dogfights at once, offering advice and warnings, while conducting an attack of his own. Like Marseille later, he was economic with his shooting, firing short bursts only. He is quoted as saying: "Once I'm in my aircraft, everything is fine. The brain is working fast, and if the enemy is met, it seems to work like a clockwork motor—accepting that, rejecting that, sizing up this, and remembering that. I have been blessed with a good pair of eyes and have learned to shoot straight. The first necessity in combat is to see the other chap before he sees you or before he gets the tactical advantage of you. The second is to hit him when you fire . . . Wait for the right moment and spar around until it arrives. Then swing in that killing punch."

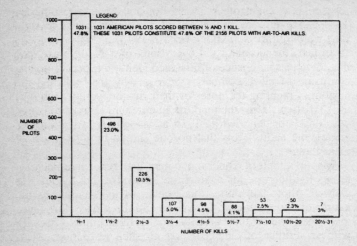

This survey splits the number of USAF 8th Air Force pilots who could claim at least a share in an air-to-air kill, into sections by score. Fairly representative of all such analyses, it also bears out the recurring figure that five percent of all pilots account for forty percent of all victories. The constant theme is that very few pilots are any good at air combat. In all, some 5,000 pilots of the 8th Air Force flew against the Germans between 1943 and 1945, although it must be admitted that for some there was no opportunity.

His style of leadership was simple, don't look now chaps, but follow me. Like many of the great fighter leaders who did not see out the war, he was brought down by ground fire, his score at 32.

As the American daylight bombing offensive on the Reich stepped up, so clever tactics and the attainment of surprise became ever more difficult, and the air defense of Germany became more and more a slugging match. Raids consisting of several hundred heavy bombers were impossible to conceal, as were the large formations of fighters, often exceeding sixty, put up against them. Gradually, long-range escort fighters began to accompany the bombers, and some really messy multi-bogey encounters took place. The American top scorer in Europe was Francis Gabreski with 31 victories, followed by Robert Johnson with 28. In all, only ten Americans achieved twenty or more victories in Europe, but one of the main reasons for this was that a fighter pilot tour of operations was restricted to 200 hours. When it is considered that an escort to Berlin took over four hours, it can be seen that the number of sorties possible was severely restricted. Johnson, with an extended tour, flew just 92 sorties. The successes achieved were again a matter of opportunities. The American fighters, ranging deep into Germany, encountered the Luftwaffe on almost every occasion, whereas the short-legged British fighters had few opportunities to score. It is difficult to pick out valid situational awareness examples from this period, as the huge multi-bogey fights made it totally impossible for any one man to keep track of what was going on around him. There are, however, some very interesting accounts from other theaters.

Surprise was not only a matter of sneaking up unobserved.

The keen-sighted Canadian George Beurling survived the war with a total of thirty-two victories. (RAF MUSEUM, HENDON)

In the early part of the Pacific War, the Zero had become a bogey to the Allies, in part due to its amazing turning ability, and in part to its very experienced Japanese Navy pilots, many of whom had fought in China. On July 22, 1942, a lone Hudson of the Royal Australian Air Force bombed the Japanese base at Buna, in New Guinea. It was then pursued by no less than six Zeros, with top scoring Japanese aces Nishizawa (87 victories), Sakai (61) and Sasai (27) among the pilots. At this point it looked no contest. Sakai takes up the story: "From a distance of 600 yards and to the rear left, I fired a burst from all four guns at the plane, hoping the Hudson would turn and allow me to lessen the distance between our two planes. [An old trick, used by Boelcke more than once.] What happened next was startling. No sooner had I fired than the Hudson went up in a steep climbing turn to the right, rolled quickly, and roared back with full speed directly at me. I was so surprised that for several moments I sat motionlesss in the cockpit. The next second every forward-firing gun in the Hudson opened up in a withering barrage. [For this moment, Sakai had lost control of the situation, and had the Hudson's shooting been as good as its flying, might well have lost his life!]

"Our Zeros scattered wildly, rolling or diving in different directions. Nothing like this had ever happened before. I caught a glimpse of Lieutenant Sasai; his jaw hung open in astonishment at the audacity of the enemy pilot. One Zero— piloted by Nishizawa, who refused to be impressed by anything—rolled out of his sudden breakaway and came down behind the bomber, his guns spitting flame.

"Again we were astounded. The Hudson heeled over in a snap roll, the fastest I had ever seen for a twin-engined plane. Nishizawa's guns sprayed only empty air . . . for nearly ten minutes we pursued the Hudson, pouring a hail of lead and explosive shells at the amazing plane. Finally a heavy burst caught the rear turret . . ."

The bomber crashed in the jungle. Realistically, there was only one outcome to an engagement of this nature, but by doing the unexpected, and very well too, the Hudson pilot made the result uncertain for a while. Had he been up against lesser pilots, or had he managed to shoot down Sakai on that

Gregory Boyington, who became the leading Marine ace in January 1944, seen here climbing into the cockpit of his F4U Corsair. (US NAVAL INSTITUTE)

first pass, or possibly damage one or two of the others, he might just have got away with it.

There were plenty of examples of the more orthodox methods of surprise. Five months later, a Wirraway of No. 4 Squadron, RAAF, based at Buna, was patrolling off the coast of New Guinea at 1,000 feet, when the pilot, John Archer, suddenly spotted a lone Zero about 2,500 feet away, and 500 feet lower. The Wirraway was derived from the Harvard trainer. Slower and less maneuverable than the Japanese fighter, it was also undergunned, having just two fixed forward-firing .303 caliber Brownings, with a single swiveling aft-facing gun operated by the observer, N. J. Muir. Archer could have been forgiven for beating a hasty retreat under the circumstances, but noting that the Japanese pilot did not appear to have seen him, he swung into a front quarter attack and fired a five-second burst. The Zero went down into the shallow water off the coast, its pilot shot through the head. In this, and many other combats, situational awareness and the lack of it enabled a David to defeat a Goliath.

A feature of the air war in the Pacific was the large number of multiple victories, combined with the fact that many aces ran up large scores in relatively few combats. Perhaps the most extreme example was Marine Lieutenant Robert Hanson of VMF-215 who, in his third operational tour, claimed 20 victories in six missions over a period of 17 days before falling to ground fire.

Many factors contribute to this phenomenon. The war in the Pacific was to a great extent composed of operations flown either from aircraft carriers or from island airfields. With carrier operations there were never enough fighters to go around, and escorts were often numerically inadequate. The defending fighters were therefore presented with a target rich environment composed mainly of bombers and torpedo aircraft. These last were mainly single engined, which made them far more vulnerable to battle damage than multi-engined types. Many operations took place over the sea at relatively long distances. This had two main effects. A severely damaged aircraft had less chance of regaining base, while the need to conserve fuel demanded economical cruising speeds, which were relatively slow, and make strike forces vulnerable to the surprise bounce. Yet another factor was that strikes generally were carried out at medium and low altitude, which tended to give defending fighters the chance to gain an altitude advantage.

Throughout the war the Japanese operated highly maneuverable but flimsy fighters, good in the dogfight but unable to absorb battle damage and survive. By contrast, the robust American fighters, with their armor and self-sealing tanks, were far more likely to survive. When later in the war new American fighters were introduced which were able to far outperform their Japanese counterparts, the dice were heavily loaded in favor of the American flyers. The legendary maneuverability of the Japanese fighters, notably the Mitsubishi Zero, flown by pilots experienced in combat against the Chinese and Russians, at first gave them an edge over Allied pilots of whatever nationality. This state of affairs was not to last long. Heavy Japanese losses, notably at Midway in June 1942 when four aircraft carriers were sunk, caused a dramatic reduction in pilot quality, which continued to reduce throughout the conflict. This, coupled with an ever increasing American technical and numerical ascendancy, saw air superiority pass irrevocably into American hands.

The leading USN and USMC scorers in the Pacific were David McCampbell and Gregory Boyington with scores of 34 and 28 respectively. As they present a great contrast in styles, we will deal with them both in turn.

David McCampbell was a most unlikely top scoring fighter pilot. A latecomer to flying, he gained his wings at the advanced age of 28. At first assigned to a fighter squadron, much of his career in naval aviation was spent as a landing signal officer, or "bats." After a spell in command of a fighter squadron, he was promoted to Air Group Commander for CAG-15 on the USS *Essex*. Most unusually, he did no combat flying as a squadron pilot, and all his impressive tally of victories were scored as Air Group Commander.

McCampbell first saw action in June 1944, at the age of 34; an old man by the standards of World War 2. Unlike many Pacific aces, McCampbell was never shot down, although on his second mission his wingman was lost and his aircraft so badly damaged by AA fire that it had to be scrapped on return to the carrier. McCampbell's next wingman was future ace Roy Rushing, who was to end the war with a score of 13 victories. Rushing's exceptional eyesight was a major factor in McCampbell's success, and his SA also seems to have been phenomenal, as he was responsible for both identification and confirmation of McCampbell's victories, while notching up a respectable score of his own. If this seems of little account, consider their most successful day.

On October 23, 1944, McCampbell led seven fighters off the *Essex* to intercept an incoming raid. About 22 miles from the task group they found 20 bombers escorted by an estimated 40 fighters. Due to a misunderstanding, five fighters

David McCampbell, the leading USN scorer in the Pacific with a score of thirty-four victories. (US NAVAL INSTITUTE)

went down on the bombers, leaving McCampbell and Rushing to deal with the large Japanese fighter force. McCampbell now takes up the story.

"The five fighters that were with my wingman and I, they went down on the bombers, and almost immediately [the Japanese fighters] went into this Lufbery. They circled around there, I guess, maybe ten or twelve minutes. At least I had time to smoke a cigarette and sit up there and watch them. We made a couple of attacks and found it was very difficult . . . we made a couple of attacks, and I think we got two planes out of that. But I didn't like it, so we just pulled up above them about 3,000 feet [approx. 18,000 feet] and watched them until they came out of the circle."

After ten minutes or so, certainly enough time for McCampbell to finish his cigarette, the Japanese fighters broke their defensive circle and turned away from the task group back toward Manila. They carried an external load, which was either a fuel tank or a bomb; David McCampbell could not be certain. While it was probably a fuel tank, the uncertainty, coupled with a pronounced lack of aggression on the part of the Japanese pilots, led McCampbell to speculate that they were not a fighter unit at all.

"I to this day think . . . that those [the Japanese fighters] must have been kamikazes, because they gave us very little fight. Two or three of them tried to climb up to [our] altitude. Of course, we picked them off in a hurry. The rest of the time, they were just sitting there flying along, taking it, and we were knocking them off right and left. Since they were headed back to Manila and away from our task group, we were in a position freely to strike them from the rear. There was no great hurry to get the leader. And we never did get him, by the way. Now the real leader was a twin engined bomber which led them in, and he was down [below]. All the bombers were behind him; the fighters were above them. But it wasn't much of a fight for us—just a question of taking your time and make sure you get one. We didn't get one every time, but we pretty well took care of them. Made 20 co-ordinated runs, and my wingman went down with me every time . . .

"We had the altitude advantage in all the time we attacked

the Japanese. We would zoom down, shoot at a plane or two. Roy and I each would take one, and I'd tell him which one I was going to take, whether it was to the right or to the left . . . We'd make an attack, pull up, keep our altitude advantage, speed, and go down again . . . In the meantime, a third pilot joined up on us, and he made, he said, two attacks, getting a plane on each one."

As the score mounted, the confusion factor was running high. David McCampbell recalled: "After Roy and I had gotten about five, I took out my pencil . . . and I started marking them down." Finally the two USN pilots broke off the action through shortage of ammunition. By this time, the fight, if it can be called that, had moved about 100 miles away from the *Essex*. McCampbell had scored nine, and Rushing five in this single action against enormous odds. Their sole damage was dents in the wing leading edges sustained from the flying debris of an exploding victim.

McCampbell's CAG-15 was in action for a total of six and a half months on this tour; rather longer than the average, which was four to five months. His total of victories was remarkable in this short span for a man who had not previously seen action. On the other hand, he was not a "fangs out, hair on fire" type. He summed up his attitude to combat as follows: "You could never know when you might run into a real topnotch fighter pilot. So I always gave them the benefit of the doubt of being a good pilot, and I engaged him in that fashion . . . There's no way you can tell whether he's good or bad until you engage him."

David McCampbell was a very professional career officer who allied his professionalism with deadly shooting ability. The award of the Congressional Medal of Honor, America's highest, precluded him from returning for a second combat tour, during which he might easily have become the Allied ace of aces.

Gregory Boyington, the USMC top scorer, was a very different character to McCampbell, and is most politely described as a hell-raiser. A Marine career officer, circumstances made a change desirable in 1941, and he joined the American Volunteer group, the Flying Tigers, in China.

Operating from Rangoon, in Burma, he downed six Japanese fighters in four hectic weeks before returning to the USA in July of that year.

Rejoining the Marine Corps, Boyington was back in action against the Japanese in September 1943, at the head of VMF-214 Black Sheep. Denied a combat assignment, he had formed the squadron from the oddments of the replacement pilot's pool, borrowed the number from a resting unit, and scrounged a complement of F4U Corsairs.

The first mission came on September 16 of that year. It was to escort bombers to a target on a Japanese held island. There was a considerable amount of cloud that day. After the bombers had delivered their load, Boyington took the Black Sheep down in search of action. It would be nice to record that his SA was top notch that day, but unfortunately that was not the case. As the Corsairs broke cloud, they found themselves in the middle of about 40 Japanese fighters which were travelling in the same direction. The surprise was total on both sides. Boyington had not even switched on his gunsight. A large dogfight developed, during which Boyington added five Zeros to his tally.

Many fruitless missions followed, until one cloudy day, after seeing the bombers safely away, Boyington took his Black Sheep back into the target area. An English speaking Japanese came up on the radio, addressing Boyington by name and asking his position. His too perfect English betrayed him. In the cat and mouse game that followed, Boyington gave his position, but was understandably about 5,000 feet too low on his altitude. The Japanese accepted the challenge and sent a formation of about 30 fighters into the area, too low and down sun. The bounce was perfect, and in a 30 second action, Boyington added another three to his score; his Black Sheep getting a further nine between them.

Boyington led another successful ruse in October, when 24 Corsairs flew over Bougainville at high altitude in bomber vics instead of fighter pairs. It should be remembered that many bombers in the theater of operations were single engined. To add another dimension to the bluff, the Corsair pilots discussed mythical bombing targets over the radio. The

Japanese responded, and committed their fighters. The Corsairs, reverting to pairs, streaked down upon them, catching them in the climb where they were slow and unhandy, hitting the leaders at about 5,000 feet and continued on down to shoot at the laggards before their wheels were retracted. Boyington claimed another three in this engagement.

By Christmas 1943, Boyington was approaching the record of 26 victories then held jointly by Rickenbacker and Marine pilot Joe Foss, and was under pressure to beat it. At about this time he encountered some Japanese Navy fighters, and commented on their much higher quality. Then on January 3, 1944, he got two more in flames, to bring his total to 28. He was shot down on this mission, in the course of a vain attempt to protect his stricken wingman, during which he ignored enemy fighters on his tail. He survived a low level bale-out by a miracle, and sat out the war in a Japanese prison camp.

In the general sense, Boyington's SA does not seem to have been of a high order, and he certainly seems to have made little enough attempt to keep the situation controllable, as did McCampbell and many others. He is notable for the ruses that he employed to reduce enemy SA, but perhaps his main claim to fame lies in his undoubted powers of leadership. Younger than McCampbell, but still old for a fighter pilot, the name "Pappy" was bestowed on him by his young pilots.

Seeing the enemy first was so important that many aces worked hard to improve their vision. George Beurling, who survived the war with a total of 32 victories, is recorded as sitting for hours, gazing into space, occasionally flicking his head to one side to stare at the wall. "See that nail on the wall?" he would say. "When I turn my head I've got to pick it up more quickly than I can think. Its a matter of training your eyes to focus swiftly, so that when you look around the sky once, you pick up anything that's out there." This paid off; Beurling knocked down no less than 27 German and Italian aircraft in just fourteen flying days over Malta. So keen and practiced was his vision that he once reported hitting a Macchi 202 five times in the cockpit area from very long range. The wreck was later found, with five holes in the cockpit. Beurling later flew over Normandy, but with little success. He was one of the pilots who was in his element flying solo or with a wingman, and could never really settle to the disciplined teamwork demanded on other fronts.

A rather similar character was Hans-Joachim Marseille, the German top scorer in North Africa, who trained his vision by staring for hours into the bright desert sun. Like Beurling, Marseille was a brilliant aircraft handler and excellent deflection shot, although he was not a long distance marksman. His skill lay in his consummate judgement of the dynamics of combat in space and time. His was an SA of a different order. By dint of constant practice, his awareness of distance and relative movement was such that he could close to within a few dozen feet of a maneuvering target, firing *when the target vanished beneath his nose,* then breaking away, leaving his wingman to keep tally on the result. His capacity for mass destruction was unrivalled, and the majority of his victories are confirmed by Allied records. His score in the desert was 151; the next German in line being Werner Schroer with 61, which was well below. He died at the height of his powers in a flying accident.

Seeing the enemy in the air was often not easy, even when ground control was steering the pilot towards them. George Barclay again: "We then went all over the upper atmosphere and apparently were very close to the Hun, but again we didn't see him. It is amazing how when one has the whole of space to search, the object searched for can pass near by without being seen, if the eyes of the searcher are focused on the distance—and the searcher cannot tell where his eyes are focused unless there are clouds, etc." Barclay was also to comment on one of his more successful colleagues: "He always seems to see his opponents crash, which I seldom do. Why?"

First things first. When there is nothing on which to focus, the eyes tend naturally to fix on a point about eighteen inches in front of the nose. Focusing one's vision at infinity, which is where it needs to be, takes training and practice. Secondly, as we have seen, some men are naturally more aware of events around them, and their concentration is such that they can keep track of what is happening. Instinct also plays a vital part. There were many recorded instances during the Second World War, but these tend to be similar to those of the earlier conflict; to recount them here would be merely repetitious.

The combination of radar coupled with air-to-air and ground-to-air radio communications had opened up a whole new dimension of SA for the day fighters. They could be directed towards the enemy at the most critical points, and once engaged, what one pilot saw could be quickly communicated to his fellows. Tactics has often been defined as a combination of fire and movement. This definition leaves out one vital point; that of communications. The more rapid, the more accurate the communications, the more effective the movement becomes which in turn increases the effectiveness of fire. The new electronic SA almost certainly tipped the scales in favor of the defenders in the Battle of Britain, and in many other encounters, specifically the Marianas Turkey Shoot in 1943, where the Japanese air assets were virtually wiped out overnight at minimal American loss. It also enabled the Luftwaffe to meet the huge American daylight raids in force, albeit with the reciprocal effect that it drew large numbers of German fighters which were mainly intent on attacking the bombers, within reach of large numbers of American fighters, at a time when attrition had seriously reduced German pilot quality. Be this as it may, the task of the detection, reporting and ground control systems was to bring the defending fighters to a point from which they could visually detect the raids themselves, after which they handled the interception. In clear visibility, a heavy bomber force could be seen at eight miles or more, rising to twenty miles if they were contrailing. This gave the ground-based detecting, reporting, and control systems a reasonable margin of error in directing the fighters. But at night, it became a whole new ballgame.

Apart from those rare exceptions when visibility was better than average, the fighter pilot had to get within 2-300 feet of his target, firstly to identify it, and secondly to shoot at it. Given the state of the art, this placed extra-ordinary demands on both the controller and the pilot. A few "cats-eye" victories were recorded in this manner, but they were insufficient to deter the bombers. The next step was to install radars in the

As World War 2 progressed, the accent almost imperceptibly started to shift to means of detection other than the human eyeball. The British AI Mk VIII is seen here mounted in a Mosquito Mk XII, the single scope display shielded from light by a visor, into which the operator was forced to peer. (IWM VIA ALFRED PRICE)

fighters, with a second crew member to operate the on-board set. This simplified the task of the controllers a bit; all they had to do now was to position the night fighter a mile or two behind the bomber, on the same heading, and at much the same altitude, until the airborne radar operator achieved contact. This, of course, was much easier said than done, but it was a step in the right direction. As the aircraft radars became more reliable, a few outstanding pilot/radar operator teams emerged on both the British and German sides. The main difficulty was that whereas in daylight the pilot could see his opponent, and know which way he was going and what he was doing, at night all the radar operator had was a blip on his screens from which he had to deduce what the target was doing. He knew where it was in azimuth and where it was in elevation, but only by watching the movement portrayed by

Radar displays were rapidly improved in the urgency of battle, depicted here is the twin scope display of the AI 10 radar. This American AI radar was easier for the operator to use, and entered service in the Mosquito NF 30 in 1944. (CROWN COPYRIGHT VIA ALFRED PRICE)

several successive scans could he make out what it was doing and where it was going. Having done this, he had to give his pilot a running commentary to guide him in to an attacking position, and this was far from easy. Very few pilot/operator teams managed more than the occasional success. This again was situational awareness, but of a different order to that of the day fighter.

As the war proceeded, so night bombing was stepped up, and so was night fighter activity. The hardware improved, as, by dint of much practice, did the operators. So successful did the night fighters become, that attempts were made to reduce their SA by electronic means. The countermeasures war, the nightly battle of the black boxes, began. This took many forms. The night fighters were never completely autonomous; they relied on GCI information to give them initial contact with the enemy. One method was to jam the ground-to-air communications, leaving the night fighters floundering about, hoping to stumble across a bomber by chance. Another, the most widely used, was to jam the radars, both ground and airborne, thus blinding the defenses.

Once again the German pilots ran up larger scores than

Early AI radars relied a great deal on the operator's skill in interpretation, and also in his ability to guide his pilot into an attacking position. The British AI Mk IV had two scopes, see left and center. The blip at far left shows the target as being a mile or so ahead and slightly lower; the one at center shows that it is also off to the right. The later AI Mk VIII used a single display scope, as seen on the right. On this can be seen three radar contacts at different levels and ranges, needing a lot of interpretative skill to sort out. Radar scopes called for a high level of SA. Incidentally, these presentations are for a fighter flying straight and level; if it banked, they would alter, considerably complicating the operator's task.

their opponents, the top-scoring German night fighter pilot being Heinz-Wolfgang Schnaufer with 121 victories. The British top scorer in defensive operations was John Cunningham with twenty. As in day operations, the opportunities for the German pilots were much greater than those for the British, and there is no reason to consider the German scores unlikely. By the time that the German night defenses reached their peak of effectiveness, the British night bombers were using radar aids to find their targets, rather as a man uses a torch on a dark night to find his path. But rather as a man using a torch shows his position to a waiting footpad, so the German fighters homed on to the bomber radars. At the same time, British intruder fighters were homing on to the German night fighter radars in their turn. But even when the British countermeasures had rendered the German radars next to useless, the night fighter pilots were not beaten. They flew to that part of the sky where the jamming was heaviest and searched visually. With the density of the bomber stream in the later stages of the war, this was almost bound to yield results.

Radar and the associated black boxes turned night fighting

from a matter of chance into an art form within the space of just four years, with spoof and feint attacks being widely used together with active jamming screens, while window could make a force of several hundred bombers appear as several thousand on the German radar sets. The aircrews learned to live with this situation, and one German pilot, who had spent some time on the Russian front, commented that night fighting was much more difficult there as the Russians were so backward that they had no radars on which to home!

Radar would also have been an advantage to the day fighters, particularly in adverse weather conditions, but the sets of the day were bulky and complex, and ideally needed a second crew member to operate them, plus a large aircraft to carry them. The night fighters were comparatively slow and unmaneuverable, and were far too vulnerable in daylight when day fighters were encountered. American Reade Tilley, an Eagle Squadron member, who scored seven victories flying with the RAF over Malta before transferring to the USAAF, came up with the following bright idea.

"While in Malta, where you could run out of wingmen right easy, I conceived the idea of a fighter tail warning device, something like a night fighter radar pointing the other way. Idea was after the initial attack when everybody had scattered, instead of having to go round up a friend (to guard your tail) you'd just switch that rascal on and keep after the Jerries. Every pilot a No. 1, was the slogan, and according to the theory we'd double the number of hunters, being everybody had their own No. 2 man built in electronically.

"At Adastral House (Air Ministry in those days) they liked the idea but thought the equipment would weigh 600 lbs., besides, rightfully they were much too busy building things they had to have and knew would work. Back in the states they were building anything people thought might work. The Air Corps Chief of Research and Development approved. A couple of PhDs at Massachusetts Institute of Technology were called in along with some RCA engineers who had been wasting their time with the impossible task of making a terrain altimeter. Turned out it worked and when pointed out the back it would tell you when somebody was coming. Best of all it weighed 20 lbs. and was the size of a shoebox." (It was later designated AN/APS-13, and with Reade Tilley as project test pilot, flying it in a P-47 Thunderbolt out of a 2,200 feet long strip, its development was a hilarious story of damaged treetops and irate farmers. Some 40,000 were eventually built.)

"Unfortunately, by the time they were installed in fighters at the front, if anybody was on our tail it was friendly. When pilots had it turned on they would often scare hell out of each other by wandering into the radar cone and setting off some poor clot's red light and klaxon horn."

As in the next chapters we move into the modern age, with electronic warning aids adding to the pilot's SA, it will be as well to remember this cautionary tale. The idea was very much a conception of its time. On Malta, the often heavily outnumbered British fighter pilots would have been greatly assisted by it. The numerical imbalance was such that nine out of every ten warnings would have been of a German fighter. By the time it reached service, its time had passed, and a more sophisticated device, preferably a passive detector, with IFF, was needed. If operated over hostile territory, the active emissions would have served as a tracking device for the enemy, and it would have been counter-productive. For the day fighter, however, it was a start in the right direction.

Chapter 4

Korea, the Last of the Gunfighters

Insofar as the Korean conflict saw the first air combat between jet fighters, it is generally regarded as the start of the modern era. This is misleading, as jet engines and swept wings notwithstanding, it was really the end of the old rather than the beginning of the new. A fighter is a weapons platform, and the weapons had not changed; they were still guns, mainly of types that had been tried and tested during World War 2. It was also the apogee of the "ever higher, ever faster" tactical trend that had commenced back in 1915, although both fighting speeds and altitudes had increased by roughly fifty percent since 1945. Nor did clever on-board electronics affect the fighting; the pilots were still dependent on their own sharpness of eye and lightness of touch.

Throughout the conflict, the MiG-15 (powered, incidentally, by a Soviet derivative of the Rolls-Royce Nene engine), had a better high altitude performance than the American F-86 Sabre, and in consequence often enjoyed the initiative conferred by position. During the conflict, improved marks of Sabre were introduced, but these merely reduced the gap rather than closing it. This made the achievements of the American fighter pilots all the more remarkable.

There are two main difficulties about fighting in the stratosphere. Firstly the air is thin; engine power falls away, and the wings give little lift. Maneuver has therefore to be gentle if formation is to be kept and altitude maintained. If hard maneuver is required, perhaps for evasion, not only does the pilot risk "dropping it," which would be embarrassing, to say the least, but there is only one way to go: downward. Secondly, visual acquisition becomes difficult. The air is very clear and the sunlight is harsh. Reflections from the cockpit onto the interior of the canopy becomes a problem. At the same time, the eyes of the pilot tend to focus on a point about eighteen inches in front of his nose, basically due to the lack of suitable external visual references. Often the only clue to the presence of other aircraft would be the occasional "flash" in the sky as the sun glinted on canopies or polished aluminum. This would tell the pilot where to look, after which "they would jump into focus," as more than one pilot put it.

A few efforts were made to reduce aircraft visibility, but a painted surface reduced speed by up to twenty knots, and the game was deemed not worth the candle. The inevitable result of this was that the vast majority of the fighting was carried out between shiny swept-winged airplanes of roughly similar appearance, which led to many cases of mistaken identity, although the short range needed for effective gunnery ensured that little damage was done to friendlies, which could be recognized long before they could be shot at. Many Sabre drivers took to carrying binoculars with them in the cockpit to ease the identification problem, while later, yellow bands were painted on in much the same manner that the Luftwaffe had used yellow noses in the earlier conflict.

While the MiG-15 was the better aircraft at high altitude, the Sabre was a match for it lower down, and had better transient performance at all levels. The Sabre was also a better gun platform. The great discrepancy in kill/loss ratios achieved by the Sabres was primarily due to superior pilot quality, higher experience levels, and better leadership. Many of the American pilots had flown in the Second World War; to name but a few, Francis Gabreski had scored 28 against the Germans and went on to notch up a further 6½ in Korea; while William Whisner, Bud Mahurin and Glen Eagleston were others. The first ace of the Korean War was, however, slow in coming. Even as the increased speeds and altitudes of World War 2 had increased the optimum shooting range compared to the first conflict, so the increased speeds and altitudes of Korea had a proportional effect on firing distances. In a nutshell, it had become ever more difficult to "stick your nose in the enemy cockpit."

The appearance of the MiG-15 in the skies over Korea came as a great shock to the West, as no other fighter could match its high altitude performance, which meant that it usually held the initiative. This is actually a Hungarian aircraft. (FLYPAST)

The first Sabres had arrived in the theater in December 1950, and five months later the first ace was still awaited. After a slow start, James Jabara, of the 334th FIS, opened his account on April 3, 1951. Nineteen days later his score stood at four, and excitement ran at fever pitch. And there he stuck, with his allotted tour of duty fast running out. The American public only half understood what the war was about, and apart from the self-esteem of the USAF, the nation needed a hero. Jabara was put up front on all the likely missions, but to no avail. Then exactly four weeks to the day after his last victory the luck changed and he scored a double to bring his score to six, after which he was sent home.

Some indication of how difficult it was to get results is shown by the fact that a further four months passed before Richard Becker and Ralph Gibson also attained ace status. But as better Sabres reached the units, the pace gradually stepped up. At the same time, tactics and teamwork were improved, with often remarkable results. Young James Low, just six months out of flight school, scored the fifth out of his eventual total of nine in June 1952, to convincingly demonstrate that a natural flair can be more effective than a high experience level. During 1953 the pace really stepped up. Mac McConnell, the top scorer of the conflict, knocked down sixteen MiGs between mid-January and mid-May of that year, while Manuel Fernandez scored 11½ during the same period to add to three that he had got earlier. Jabara, returning for a further tour of duty, added nine to his tally between mid-May and mid-July of that year, a period of just eight weeks.

Korea had also seen the demise of the large fighter formation, which was found to be too unwieldy at high speeds and even more so at high altitudes. The basic fighter formation was the four, made up of two pairs. The practice was to saturate the area with flights of four, which could then give each other mutual support. On the other hand, reliance on the human eyeball was insufficient, and rules were evolved to extract maximum effect from the aircraft involved. The most remarkable of these and certainly the most comprehensive, and which became for many year the fighter pilot's bible, was *No Guts, No Glory,* by Major (later Major-General) Frederick (Boots) Blesse, who shot down nine MiG-15s and one propeller-driven La-9 during the conflict. Space precludes printing the entire work, but the author is indebted to *USAF Fighter Weapons Review* for permission to quote large extracts from it. Only some of the background material has been omit-

The F-86 Sabre gained most of its enviable reputation in the skies over Korea, fighting the MiG-15. Its success was mainly due to pilot quality. In Pakistan Air Force service against India in 1965, about a quarter of the Sabres carried Sidewinders, and the Indian fighters opposing them were forced to assume that they were faced with missile-carrying aircraft until it could be proved otherwise. This badly limited the tactics they could use. (PAKISTAN AIR FORCE)

ted, and the essential material is all reproduced in the Appendix (see p. 193).

In *No Guts, No Glory,* certain themes are recurrent. The concept of mutual support is perhaps over-riding. Two men can see more than one, and four can see more than two. The flight leader is the striker, and both his wingman and the second element are where possible used to protect him. Much stress is laid on keeping all flight members aware of the situation at all times, while survival is also given high priority. This possibly accounts for Korea being a relatively "safe" war in terms of fighter combat compared with many World War 2 campaigns. It also accounts for the comparatively low victory per 100 sorties ratio achieved by the Sabres. With each flight of four aircraft being made up of one shooter and three protectors, the offensive capability was reduced by a fair margin. On the other hand, the low loss ratio sustained by the Sabres throughout the conflict justifies this operational philosophy.

What *No Guts, No Glory* really did was to lay down ground rules for combat in a manner never before attempted. It said to the novice pilot, this is what we expect of you and basically this is how to do it. Here are most of the situations in which you can expect to find yourself, and this is how the

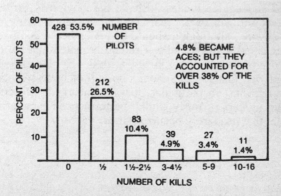

This histogram examines opportunity as a factor in the records of 800 USAF Sabre pilots, each of whom flew at least 25 counter-air missions. Over half the total number of pilots failed to score, and less than one in twenty made ace, despite having sufficient opportunities.

situation should develop. Having studied and absorbed the article, the young pilot could then, provided that he could keep his cool, both see the situation at the outset and anticipate what was going to happen. Thus armed, he was better equipped to survive and gain practical experience. Perhaps the most effective ploy described is the attack designed to split off support element from lead element, or wingman from leader by using an attacking line best suited to a switch of targets at the last moment. This is a classic example of a ruse intended to present a picture of events as they are not to the enemy, who if he falls for it, at first thinks that he has SA, only to discover within seconds that he has not. The other interesting exhortation is to assume every adversary is the world's best until he shows that he is not. This shows a surprisingly cautious, if very professional attitude, with the unposed question, "does the other guy know something that I don't?" A final very practical comment was "If you are going to shoot him down, you have to get in there and mix it up with him." The wartime sky is a dangerous place, and despite all efforts to minimize the risks, it will remain so, if worthwhile results are to be obtained.

It is also noticeable that in the discussion of selection of leaders, flying ability comes well down the list, after results in combat and aggressiveness. Blesse has obviously arrived at Mannock's truism of 35 years earlier, that good flying never killed anyone, although it should be remembered that bad flying has killed many. Finally it should be noted that *No Guts, No Glory* was written specifically with the Korean experience in mind, and that some, although not all, of its lessons are no longer relevant. In particular, it was concerned with combat between fighters of fairly similar performance characteristics, an event that has rarely occurred since.

Chapter 5

Avionics and Missiles

Originally there had been two main types of fighters. The first, intended for daylight, clear weather use, had typically been single-engined and single-seat. It was small, fast and agile, with good acceleration and a high rate of climb. Gun-armed, it relied on a combination of ground control and visual detection by the pilot to find its quarry. The second was more an interceptor than a fighter, and was designed to operate at night or in adverse weather conditions. Aided by ground control, it carried an on-board radar, which in most cases needed a second crew member to operate it. While in the defensive case the day fighter could be held on the ground until the time came to scramble, the night fighter ideally needed to be put on patrol. To be effective, it was required to have long endurance. The bulk of the radar, especially in the days of thermionic valves, and the need to carry a second crew member, called for a large aircraft, which in turn needed two engines to give the necessary performance, which in turn called for a large amount of fuel to give the necessary endurance. The result was inevitably a compromise, with performance and agility being traded for the other needs of the mission.

Heavy fighters had been extensively used during the Second World War, and had been very successful at night, and in daylight against unescorted bomber formations. But when they had encountered the fast and agile day fighters, they had been hacked down in droves, having neither the speed nor the agility to survive. As a result they had been relegated to night or adverse weather operations. Of course, the converse was also true. A day fighter, flying at night, dependent only on its pilot's vision, backed up by ground control, was very much at the mercy of the radar-equipped night fighter. Ideally what was needed was a fighter which could combine the better qualities of both types; that could operate equally effectively by day or by night, in fair weather or foul. This objective was effectively hampered by the available technology, which did not permit the combination, until the 1950s, when quantum leaps in all areas moved the dream into the realms of possibility.

The most important advance came in the field of propulsion, where new high temperature alloys allowed more efficient engine design, and the development of afterburning raised the level of available power by a tremendous amount. Within a few short years, maximum speeds doubled, from the barely supersonic to the bisonic. Far more to the point, there was sufficient power available to allow the designers to package a large radar and two crewmen into an airframe big enough to accommodate them, and still produce a fighter that lacked nothing in performance against its single seater counterpart, although inevitably maneuverability suffered a bit.

At much the same time, the transistor appeared, which made airborne radars lighter and more compact, to say nothing of increasing their reliability. A simple radar could now be shoehorned into the nose of even the smallest fighter to increase the search ability of the pilot to far beyond normal visual range, although naturally they did not have the capacity of the larger and more exotic pieces of kit. The radar-equipped simple day fighter was enthusiastically described as having "limited" all-weather capability, although marginal would be a more accurate term. But however limited the radars, they marked a definite shift in emphasis toward increasing SA by electronic means.

Equally dramatic advances were being made in weaponry. As speeds increased—and this applied to bombers as well as fighters—so the aircraft gun became potentially less effective. Many all-weather interceptors during the late 1940s and early '50s carried batteries of unguided rockets to deal with the fast, high flying bomber, but these were ineffective against fighters in maneuver combat. Under development was a whole new family of homing rockets which used either semi-active radar homing on a target illuminated by the fighter's radar, or infra-red homing onto the heat emitted by the engine of the target. These new weapons could maneuver in flight to follow their targets.

As a result of this technology explosion, it was widely predicted that close range maneuver combat had gone forever, and that the only type of manned fighter needed was the interceptor, able to detect and destroy targets far beyond visual distance. In some quarters, notably the British Government in 1957, it was even believed that the manned interceptor would

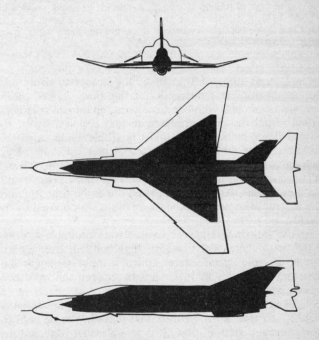

The most basic form of situational awareness is visual, and in close combat the size of the aircraft can be critical, as a small aircraft will remain invisible for far longer than a large one. To illustrate the point, here we have the silhouette of MiG-21 superimposed on that of an F-4E Phantom. Where visual acquisition is concerned, the MiG driver has a distinct advantage, being able to see the Phantom from a distance at which he is still invisible.

While the Mirage III gained a superb reputation in Israeli service in 1967 and 1973, it did not do so well in PAF service against India in 1971. Once again pilot quality proved to be the dominant factor in air combat. (PAKISTAN AIR FORCE)

be supplanted within a few years by the surface-to-air missile. The outlook for the fighter pilot at this time seemed bleak. How was he to cope with combat against an unseen enemy far beyond visual distance, armed with and opposed by (if the boffins were to be believed) almost infallible guided missiles? Was air combat really to become a matter ruled by clever electronics, with the pilot cast as a mere button pusher? Was it really to become a case of "may the best black boxes win?" This view seems terribly naïve today, but at the time it gained wide currency. Let us examine the realities, as opposed by the theory.

Firstly, the Mach 2 speeds, which were desirable to allow the fighter to intercept the fast and high bomber, were a bit of a myth. Bisonic speeds were attainable only at height altitudes; the denser air at lower levels reduced the maximum velocity attainable considerably, typically to Mach 1.1 at sea level. Even up high, it took forever for the fighter to attain Mach 2, and used so much fuel that it could not be held for any significant length of time. It is also a matter of record that many fighters theoretically capable of attaining Mach 2 have been unable to do so due to the fuel gauge needle dropping faster than the Machmeter needle could rise. From a practical point of view, if the fighter was to have any worthwhile endurance at all, it was forced to cruise at a high subsonic speed, only using after-burner for acceleration, combat, and disengagement. Blesse, in *No Guts, No Glory,* stressed the importance of keeping a close check on the fuel gauge. The use of afterburning made this injunction far more critical.

Neither was radar quite the panacea that had been supposed. It was great for picking up targets at long range, but tended to be erratic in performance. Much depended on target size, aspect, and radar reflectivity. For example, an early Phantom radar could detect a Tu-20 bomber at more than thirty miles, but it was hard-pressed to detect the small MiG-21 from head on at more than a dozen miles or so, and even then there was a considerable difference between detection, and the lock-on needed to launch a homing missile. While radar was, and still is, a valuable aid, and can expand the pilot's SA bubble to a considerable distance, its "look" is very limited. Typically it extends sixty degrees to either side of the aircraft centerline, and can at most cover no more than five or six degrees in elevation, although this can be trained either up or down. This leaves an awful lot of blind area, while initially, look down was essentially nonexistent before pulse Doppler radar came on the scene, and limited after it, with not a few blind spots caused by particular target speeds and crossing angles. Furthermore, as had been hardly learned in World War 2, radar was vulnerable to countermeasures, and could be jammed and spoofed. Finally, radar is an emission on which an enemy can home, a beacon which betrays the fighter's presence and possibly even its purpose.

Finally we have the new wonder missiles, which in sterile laboratory-like conditions performed admirably on the test range, giving kill probabilities of between eighty and ninety percent. These also had their problems, notably with seeker head sensitivity and look angles, fuzing, and reliability. Often the seeker head sensitivity was less than the theoretical maximum launch range, while a wildly evading target could often get outside the gimbal limits of the head and break the lock-on. Heat homers were intrinsically accurate, but could not see through cloud or heavy rain, and were easily distracted by alternative heat sources, such as the sun reflecting off snow. The less accurate but longer ranged SARH missiles ran into difficulties over positive target identification at beyond visual range, and were rarely used as intended. Fuzing was also a

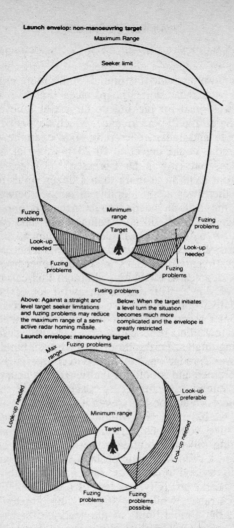

Launch envelop: non-manoeuvring target

Maximum Range

Seeker limit

Minimum range

Target

Fuzing problems

Look-up needed

Fuzing problems

Fuzing problems

Look-up needed

Fuzing problems

Fusing problems

Above: Against a straight and level target seeker limitations and fuzing problems may reduce the maximum range of a semi-active radar homing missile.

Below: When the target initiates a level turn the situation becomes much more complicated and the envelope is greatly restricted.

Launch envelope: manoeuvring target

Max range

Fuzing problems

Look-up needed

Look-up preferable

Minimum range

Target

Look-up needed

Fuzing problems

Fuzing problems possible

A missile launch envelope is quite a complicated thing, and range is almost infinitely variable, depending on a combination of missile performance, altitude, relative between shooter and target, relative speeds of shooter and target, and seeker head limitations. Above is shown the envelope for a non-maneuvering target, while below is the envelope for a maneuvering target, in which it can be seen that maneuver reduces the optimum firing areas quite dramatically.

problem. Proximity fuzes were used, set to detonate a fixed time after contact was made. The slight delay inbuilt was to allow a tail aspect missile time to overhaul the target and explode in an area where lethal damage might be expected to ensue. From head-on, the same setting would take the missile partly down the length of the target aircraft. From the beam, however, it could easily pass before detonating, doing little or no damage. When the shooting wars started, it was also found that the new weapons were a little delicate for the rough and tumble of operational life, and were unreliable in consequence.

Even when working as advertised, the missiles had their limitations. They could generally not be launched below a certain aircraft speed or above a certain g loading, which reduced their effectiveness in maneuver combat. They had minimum launch limits of the order of half a mile or so, which was the time taken for them to arm and commence tracking. Ground clutter could confuse the seeker heads if the target was below them. They were accelerated to high speed shortly after launch, after which they were just coasting, losing both speed and maneuver capability, until toward the end of their run, they could neither catch a high speed target, nor maneuver to follow even a gently evading one. The brochure figures issued were truthful in a static situation, but made meaningless by the dynamics of combat. From head-on, the maximum range was limited by the sensitivity of the seeker head, while from astern it was severely curtailed by the speed of the target. Altitude also makes a significant difference. At sea level, a missile may only have one third the range that it has at high altitude, and its maximum speed at burnout is also reduced more than a little.

After due consideration, we may assume that life for the fighter pilot was not as hopeless as it once appeared; just rather more difficult. Neither radar nor missiles were infallible. What they actually did was to expand the SA "bubble" in which the pilot needed to know what was happening in order to fight successfully, to well beyond visual limits. In order to know how well he coped, we need to look at some of the limited wars that were fought over the next two decades.

There are two important areas to examine; the various

Arab/Israeli conflicts, culminating in the Bekaa Valley in 1982, and the protracted war in South-East Asia between 1965 and 1973. The Middle Eastern wars are marked by short duration, high intensity fighting in the air, while in South-East Asia, the United States air services, Air Force, Navy, and Marine Corps to a lesser degree, tried to carry out a strategic bombing campaign using tactical aircraft over a period of many years against a practiced combination of air and ground defenses in North Vietnam, while hamstrung by political considerations. Perhaps here is a good place to dispose of the old canard, that Vietnam was a "political" war. So has been every other war in history; war being merely a brute force extension of policy.

Almost without exception, the Middle Eastern air battles were fought out in daylight in fine weather and cloudless skies, conditions which aided visual detection. Equally the Israeli pilots seem to have come off best by a handsome margin. If asked why, the usual response is that they have the best aircraft, and that their pilot selection and training methods are better than those of other nations. There is of course an element of truth in this, although until comparatively recent times the element of superiority in their aircraft was marginal, if it existed at all. As to pilot selection, there is simply no way of knowing, but in the area of training there can be no doubt that they are better than their Arab opponents, and very good by any standards. What is certain is that Israeli fighter pilots have more air combat experience than those of any other nation, and never in the last thirty years have they had to go to war without the benefit of battle-hardened leaders. Although the wars in which they have fought have been of short duration, the intervals have been full of intermittent skirmishing, which has kept them sharp. In one respect, however, they are no different to the fighter pilots of any other nation. They have a small proportion of flyers who consistently do well in the air combat arena while the remainder do not. Their current ranking ace is G–, with seventeen victories. Israel is much more coy about names and specifics than most, but certain details have emerged about their exploits. They are also reluctant to release firm figures, and a little detective work is necessary.

The Six Day War of 1967 commenced with the now famous pre-emptive strike on Egyptian air bases. While this did not, as is sometimes thought, take out the EAF entirely, it reduced them to more manageable proportions, as prior to the outbreak of hostilities Israel had been heavily outnumbered as well as being surrounded by hostile nations. Notwithstanding the success of the counter-air strikes, a considerable amount of air fighting took place resulting in claimed victories of 58 against admitted losses of three. The first figure is remarkable in that all victories were scored with the gun, at a time when both the Matra R530 and Shafrir I missiles were not only available, but used. While neither was terribly reliable or very effective, one would expect better results than this. The R530 had claimed its first, and as far as is known only, kill, an Egyptian MiG-19, the previous November. That the Shafrir was used during the Six Day war there can be no doubt.

On the morning of June 6, four Iraqi Tu-16s took off from Habbaniyah to attack Netanya. Of these, two returned shortly after, a third landed at H3, and only the fourth, reported as being piloted by the bomber unit commander, carried on. After bombing Netanya it continued toward Ramat David Air Base, near which it was intercepted by a Mirage which damaged it with a Shafrir I. Immediately after, it was badly hit by anti-aircraft gunfire and crashed at the emergency landing strip at Meggido. The first kill by a Shafrir I came within five weeks of the end of the war when an Egyptian MiG-21 was downed. The Arab fighters were missile armed with the AA-2 Atoll; there can be no possible doubt that the Israeli fighters also carried and used missiles; therefore the claim that all the victims of the Israeli fighters fell to cannon fire seems rather odd. The admitted Israeli losses in air/air is demonstrably inaccurate. After Iraqi Hunters had raided targets in the Izrael Valley on the morning of June 5, three Vautours were sent from Ramat David to attack the Hunter base at H3. They were intercepted by two MiG-21s and evaded two Atolls which were launched at them. This rather messed up the attack, although the Vautours survived unscathed, and a further strike was scheduled for the following day.

As the Iraqi Tu-16 referred to earlier overflew Ramat David, four Vautours took off, escorted by two Mirages. As the Israeli force neared H3, they encountered MiG-21s and Hunters, and a battle royal developed, in which the Mirage leader, believed to have been Yoram Agmon, shot down a MiG-21 and a Hunter, while a second Hunter fell to the guns of the Vautour No 3, Ben-Zion Zohar. Successful though the air acton was, the counter-air strike was less so, and a third attack was launched on the morning of June 7, intended to close down H3. The force for the third strike was composed of one Vautour IIN leading three Vautour IIAs, escorted by four Mirage IIICJs, which were flown by Ezra Dothan, Gideon Dror, David Porat and Reuben Har-el. The Jordanian Marconi 242 radar station at Ajlun had been hard hit on the previous day, and was believed to be out of action, but nevertheless, the ingress to H3 was flown at low level in an attempt to avoid detection. This failed, and the intruders were bounced by eight Iraqi Hunters as they approached the target. Breaking into the attack, Gideon Dror latched onto the tail of a Hunter, only to have another drop in behind him in the classic "daisy chain." Ezra Dothan tried to intervene, but was too late; Dror's Mirage was fatally hit and he was forced to eject, although his conqueror followed him down in short order, the victim of Dothan's guns. Two Vautours, including the strike leader, were also shot down by the Hunters. This third and last raid was a failure, and furthermore three Israeli aircraft were lost for one Iraqi.

The saga of the raids on H3 has been recounted for two reasons; firstly to show that on at least one occasion in this rather one-sided air war they were on the losing side, and against a demonstrably inferior fighter too, and secondly to back up the claim that the admitted air-to-air losses of the Israeli Air Force were inaccurate. Here we have three losses in a single action. The loss of two Mystére IVAs had also been admitted, while a Mirage pilot ran himself out of fuel while downing an Egyptian MiG-21; he was recovered but his machine was lost. The conclusions to be drawn at this point are simple; while the Israeli pilots were of high quality and well trained, the fighting was not quite the walkover that was presented at the time. The Israeli attitude is, of course, understandable: ringed by hostile neighbors, they would one day have to fight again, and the psychological advantage of having their pilots presented as supermen was well worth a little inaccuracy. It can be regarded as pilot SA raised to a national level.

A little desultory skirmishing followed the Six Day War, and it was not until June 1969 that the fighting flared up again, in the so-called War of Attrition, which was to last until August 1970. Hostilities started with Egyptian artillery fire at Israeli positions across the Suez Canal, which provoked Israeli retaliatory air attacks. GCI played an increasingly important part at this time, and ECM apart, deception became a standard part of the fighter formation armory. As the Soviet Colonel V. Dubrov commented in *Aviatsiya i kosmonavtika* in April 1978:

". . . utilization of natural conditions for concealment was sometimes practically impossible. This was the case in the Near East, characterized by predominantly flat terrain and cloudless skies. Under these conditions principal attention was focused on efficient formation of fighter groups prior to engagement . . . Approach formation was compact, the groups close to one another, the aircraft positioned with minimum spacings and intervals. Freedom of maneuver was limited in the interest of observing radar concealment. They were counting not on the enemy failing to spot fighters in the air, but on preventing the enemy from promptly figuring out the engagement intentions. On the radar screens the close-packed formations was observed only as a single blip. And therefore the observer was unable to determine the character of deployment of enemy forces or the adversary's plan."

Part of situational awareness consists of knowing the strengths and limitations of the aircraft/weapons systems employed, and towards the end of the War of Attrition an interesting multiple combat occurred that illustrates this point. On May 12, 1970, two A-4H Skyhawks were scrambled to "Patachland," a zone to the west of Mount Hermon at the time under PLO control, to support the ground troops. The leader was Ezra Dothan, by this time a squadron commander. The decision had earlier been taken to fit all Skyhawks with 30 mm DEFA cannon in place of the standard 20 mm M20s, but at this time, Dothan's aircraft was the only one so fitted. Other armament carried was air-to-ground rockets.

Circling the battlefield, trying to pick out enemy from friendly forces in difficult terrain, Dothan's No 2 called MiG-17s below, and was given the lead to attack. The wingman missed, and following up, Dothan launched a pod of rockets at a MiG, but they fell short. He adjusted his aim to well above and launched a second salvo, blasting the MiG-17 from the sky, then broke furiously as two more '17s came in from astern, guns blazing. Failing to nail him, they split for home, leaving the two Skyhawks with one solitary MiG-17. With plenty of fuel left, Dothan felt confident enough to tell two supporting Mirages, "find yourself another," and continued to fight. The MiG pilot had been using afterburner for several minutes, and Dothan guessed that he would be low on fuel, and so kept after him, eventually bringing his guns to bear for a killing burst. These two victories were the only ones attributed to the Skyhawk in Israeli service.

The same day and in the same area, two Mirages flown by established aces Amos Amir and Asher Snir (who died of cancer in 1986 as the Israeli second highest scorer) were on patrol when Amir sighted a solitary MiG-17 at very low level to the west of Mount Hermon. As they sneaked rapidly in behind, the thought, quickly suppressed, crossed Snir's mind that the contest was too unequal; two Mirages flown by experienced and successful pilots against one MiG-17. They were to be surprised. As the Mirages closed to gun range, the MiG-17 broke hard, dropped to ground level, and put on a superlative display of defensive flying over the next 8½ minutes, during which time Snir fired only three bursts of cannon fire and Amir about the same, all of which missed. The Mirages carried early Sidewinders, the AIM-9B, and Snir had frequently got a tone on one of his, indicating that it had acquired a target. However, he had been one of the pilots who had carried out the acceptance trials on the weapon, and he was aware of its limitations. It could not be launched at a lower target as it was likely to home on the hot ground; it

Asher Snir, Israel's second highest scoring ace.

could not be launched from very low level, as immediately after firing it sinks below the aircraft before commencing to guide, and at the levels that this combat was fought, would have impacted the ground after launch; and finally, it could not be launched at load factors exceeding 2½g. Despite the seeker head acquiring the target, satisfactory launch conditions just could not be achieved. Just as he was about to eject for a frustration light, Snir noticed that the Syrian pilot was about to cross a wider than usual valley. Leaving Amir trying yet another abortive gun attack, Snir gained a few hundred feet, closing to 800 m as he did so, and with his Sidewinder growling, he squeezed the trigger even before the Syrian crossed the near edge of the valley. The missile sank after launch, just clearing the valley edge, then stabilized and homed in, ripping off the right wing of the MiG-17.

These two accounts are of interest primarily because of the understanding they show of the weapon characteristics. In the first instance, an attack aircraft knocked down a fighter with a weapon never remotely intended for the task, while in the second, a pilot with less knowledge of the weapons limitations would have launched (and wasted) his Sidewinder far earlier.

In October 1973 hostilities flared again when Egyptian forces crossed the Suez Canal in concert with a heavy attack by Syria on the Golan Heights. Air combat reached a new level of intensity, with multi-bogey incursions by both sides. The confusion level was high, and not a few "own goals" were scored by both sides, a factor which led the Israelis to identify their aircraft with large yellow or orange triangles outlined in black on the wings and tail surfaces to aid identification at close quarters. Claims and counter-claims are as usual, confusing. The Israelis originally claimed a total of 335 victories for the loss of either four or six, but this has since been scaled down to 277 victories, which is still quite impressive, while some sources state that their losses in air combat amounted to twenty out of a total loss of 103. In this conflict, only about sixty Arab aircraft fell to cannon fire; the rest were brought down by missiles, the Shafrir 2/Mirage and Neshr combination accounting for 102, while at least 36 victories were claimed with the Sidewinder/Phantom combination. It is possible that this last figure is on the low side, as it is believed that the medium-ranged Sparrow saw little usage in this conflict, and this is the only weapon unaccounted for. Phantom pilot Israel Baharav was the top scorer of the conflict with fourteen victories, thirteen of them scored in two days. The Israelis made considerable use of ECM and AEW during the war, which gave them a distinct advantage over their adversaries, but the victory/loss ratio obtained is still remarkable, even if the least favorable figures are used. It should of course be stated that Hosni Mubarak, currently the President of Egypt, but at the time the Commander in Chief of the Egyptian Air Force, has issued a strong refutation of the accuracy of the Israeli figures, but this notwithstanding does not deny an Israeli victory in the air war.

Meanwhile, on the far side of the world, the Americans had become embroiled in a war against North Vietnam which was to last from 1965 until January 1973. Air fighting was sporadic, arising from North Vietnamese attempts to hinder the deep penetration strikes made by the Americans in the north of the country. On paper it was a mismatch, the might of the USA against a small and impoverished country, albeit backed and supplied by the USSR and China. North Vietnam rarely possessed more than about 100 fighters, mainly MiG-17s and -21s, with a few Shenyang F.6s later on. Against this, the USA could field a formidable array of attack aircraft, protected in the main by F-4 Phantom escorts. The USAF strike forces were based mainly in Thailand, well out of harm's way, while the USN operated from aircraft carriers in the Gulf of Tonkin. So far it was David versus Goliath, but there were other factors evening up the air fighting. The first was the sheer density of the ground defenses, radar-directed guns and surface-to-air missiles. This has been presented as the most effective air defense in history, but while this is overstating the case, it could be deadly, and had to be taken very seriously indeed if unacceptable losses were not to be incurred. The weather was poor for much of the year, and this also worked to the advantage of the defenders. As if this was not bad enough, the American flyers labored under self-imposed handicaps, such as target restrictions which placed the MiG bases off limits for much of the war, prohibited attacks on the SAM 2 sites unless they fired first for quite a time, and established a "Tom Tiddler's Ground" within thirty miles of the Chinese border, thereby providing a sanctuary for the MiGs when the going got rough.

Nor could the Americans utilize the factor of surprise to any great extent. USN strikes were launched from carriers in the Gulf of Tonkin, about 200 miles off the coast, and generally headed straight in at medium altitudes. The USAF, based in Thailand, over 500 miles away from Hanoi, was in much worse case. The distance to be covered made in-flight refuelling a necessity, and this was generally done at high altitude over Laos or Cambodia, in full view of the North Vietnamese radars. From this point, there were only two routes used to the North; out over the sea and back over the coast near Haiphong, or the more usual track up to the forbidden line near the Chinese border, then down the line of mountains known as "Thud Ridge," which offered a modicum of screening from the ground detection system. The strike forces were therefore fairly predictable in their routing, only the exact target being unknown to the North Vietnamese. For defensive screening the Americans were forced to rely almost entirely on chaff screens and ECM jamming aircraft. For offensive work they received limited assistance from AEW aircraft and a radar cruiser stationed in the Gulf of Tonkin, but in the main they were dependent on their organic systems and the alertness of their flyers. Losses were high, the majority caused by radar-directed guns and many more by SAMs, with relatively few falling to fighters, although this did not mean that the air threat could be taken lightly.

It soon became obvious that the victory/loss ratio achieved over Korea was not being repeated, and at times was in fact adverse. There were a variety of reasons for this. Firstly, the main American fighter, the F-4 Phantom, was not suitable for close combat, and nor were its weapons. It was far bigger than its Soviet-designed adversaries, and could be seen from much greater distances, which gave the MiG drivers an advantage at visual ranges. Secondly its wing loading was high, and although it could turn with a MiG-21 at high transonic speeds, it lost out badly in a turning fight when the speed bled off. Thirdly, the tight Soviet-style GCI used by the NVAF tended to be more effective than the Phantom's on-board radar. Fourthly, for a long time the Phantom carried no gun, which meant it had no close range weapon for use within about 2,500 ft. Fifthly, the American wonder missiles often failed to work as advertised. Finally there is the often overlooked fact that American pilot quality was often not all that it might have been.

If this statement seems heretical, consider that firstly, American fighter pilots were not trained in air combat to any great degree, as the new era of wonder missiles was popularly supposed to have made maneuver combat irrelevant. The war that USAF pilots of the period were training for was a "worse case" scenario involving intercepting fast high bombers, and delivering tactical nuclear weapons at high speed and low level. Air combat did not really enter into it. Secondly, there was a pilot shortage which was aggravated by the fact that for the first few years, the back seater in a Phantom was a rated pilot, which required double the number of rated pilots. There was also a rule which said that everybody had to complete one tour before anybody started a second. Fair minded but not very practical, this created a situation where a redundant tanker driver, after a short period of retraining, could find himself holding the pole of a F-4 in the big league. These "SAC Retreads" as they were known, generally acquitted themselves well in that they could fly the mission, deliver the ordnance, and generally get themselves back home, but they could hardly be expected to perform well in the air combat arena, in which even the dedicated air combat jockeys were having difficulties.

We have touched on the shortcomings of the Phantom, but this was not a one way street. It also had some very good points. It was fast, long legged by the standards of the day, and very rugged. It was twin-engined, which gave a measure of redundancy, and had a two-man crew, which was made necessary by the complexity of the radar and avionic systems. When the backseater was not crouched over the scope, he could take his head out of the office and check the vulnerable rear quadrant. Some forty percent of visual sightings in Vietnam were made by the guy in the back, which greatly increased the SA of the crew as a whole. He became in practice a wingman in very close formation.

The years of air fighting over North Vietnam produced just two pilot aces, both Phantom drivers, with three backseaters also making the grade. There was also one "very nearly" who could so easily have been the top scorer of the entire conflict. Those who became aces did it in 1972, which was the final full year of the war. The "very nearly" was the legendary Robin Olds, who flew in the early years.

Colonel (as he was then) Olds was one of the very few World War 2 fighter aces still in a combat position, and is generally regarded as *the* fighter pilot of the war by those who knew him. His score during the conflict was two MiG-21s and

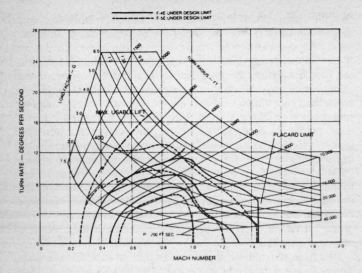

Currently a fighter pilot is expected to know the flight regimes where his aircraft is superior to that of his opponent, and also to be able to estimate his opponent's energy state just by watching him. This is a comparison of turn performance at 15,000 ft. between an F-4E Phantom (solid line), and an F-5E Tiger II (broken line).

two MiG-17s, and as we shall see, this score might possibly have been doubled with just a little luck. He was one of the few who had the ability to keep track of what was going on around him at all times, as one who flew with him records.

Lieutenant Colonel Bill Lafever, now retired, was posted to backseating in Phantoms immediately after completing pilot training, as were all of his classmates. Posted to the famous "Triple Nickel" 555th TFS, which was part of the 8th TFW based at Korat in Thailand, he flew backseater to Robin Olds on several occasions, and in the same flight on many others. On May 4, 1967, the 8th TFW provided two flights of Phantoms as MIGCAP for five flights of Thuds of the 355th TFW. One flight of Phantoms was positioned midway down the strike force, while the other, led by Olds, brought up the rear, the position from which the MiGs were most likely to attack. The Phantom flight, callsign Flamingo, was a distinguished one, containing three future Generals; Olds himself, Dick Pascoe (two victories) on his wing, and Bill Kirk in the No 3 slot, also to gain two victories in Vietnam. The fourth man was Norman Wells. Coming down Thud Ridge, near Phuc Yen airfield, two MiG-21s came in from the left, closing on the rearmost flight of Thuds. Bill Lafever, from his vantage point in the backseat of Olds' Phantom, takes up the story.

"Pascoe, our No 2 on the right side, called two MiGs at ten o'clock. Olds says 'OK, I got 'em.' So we do a vector roll attack and the MiGs did a defensive split. We followed one and launched two Sparrows at him. One went ballistic; the other passed behind and failed to detonate. The MiG was really hauling about, and we hassled with him for a good five minutes every which way, upside down, all the good things. We fired three Sidewinders at him, one of which went off just under his tailpipe and started a fire, but he kept going. While all this was going on, the other MiG had extended out, then came back. I picked him coming back over us. I said 'We got the other MiG twelve o'clock high!' Olds says 'I got him.' He knew; he actually *knew* where the other MiG was in the middle of all the hassle. That's SA. How do you teach a thing like that?"

The MiG-21, the second of Olds' eventual tally of four crashed on Phuc Yen airfield, witnessed by Bill Kirk. Some time later, Bill Lafever was flying backseat in the No 3 spot of a flight led by Olds. In the front seat was a "SAC retread," an ex-KC-135 driver, inexperienced in jet combat.

"Normally, when the MiGs, were up, they were up; there were MiGs everywhere. We started an engagement, and Olds was hassling with two MiG-17s, about 10,000 ft. below us. I had locked onto a MiG, and I am looking at him through the window at about ten o'clock. I said over the intercom, 'shoot, shoot the son of a bitch.' The guy in front wouldn't shoot. He said. 'Olds is down there.' I look up, and there is a MiG-17 coming over the top, and I said 's***', we got one rolling in on us.' No sweat, there was a Thud right on his ass. They came by close. I could see both the guys in their cockpits, the color

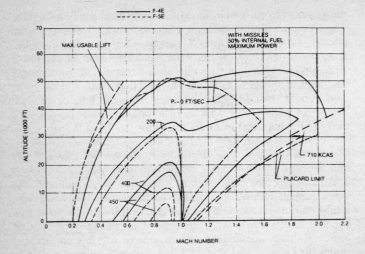

Energy management varies considerably at different altitudes as well as between different aircraft. Here are shown the specific excess power contours for the F-4E (solid line) and F-5E (broken line). Specific excess power, usually noted as P_s, determines the maneuver capability available, and whether height has to be traded for speed, or energy for turning capability. At zero P_s, maneuver will cause loss of speed, loss of altitude, or both. The modern fighter pilot must retain an awareness of his energy state at all times.

of their helmets, and the F-105 is really a strafer, standing on his nose and spewing 20 mm at the MiG-17, which is hit. They go on down. Olds, who is way down below, still hassling with two MiGs, calls on the radio 'nice shot, that!' It's unbelievable, but he knew what was going on."

Robin Olds, who commanded the 8th TFW, based at Ubon, Thailand, between September 30, 1966 and September 22, 1967, welded it into a highly effective unit which downed more MiGs than any other during his tour of duty. His own comments on success in aerial combat were as follows:

"The key is what you can see, retain, anticipate, estimate in a three-dimensional movement of many aircraft. Can you look at an enemy aircraft and know the odds—to get him before someone else—if he can get behind you first, and so on? Its a three dimensional impression; you must get it in seconds. This is essential in aerial combat. The guy you don't see will kill you. You must act instantly, anticipate the other fellow's motives, know that when you do this, he must do one of several things."

Bill Lafever rates Olds as the greatest fighter leader of the war. The Deputy Commander Operations at Ubon at this time was Daniel "Chappie" James, also destined to make General. Bill Lafever recalls:

"Chappie was a great PR man. He could fire you up. In fact, he spoke at my graduation from pilot training, and I walked out of chapel wanting to kill people! He was more of a pusher. By contrast, Robin Olds led from the front. His style was more laid back, 'follow me guys, we're going on package 6, and probably some of us ain't coming back, but I'm going to be up there leading you.' And to me, that's leadership."

Like Jabara in the Korean War, Olds came under pressure to get the magic five, and in fact was very unlucky not to. But with him, leadership came before getting five red stars painted on the intake splitter plate. Bill Lafever flew with him at a time when his score was four. The 8th TFW were MIGCAP covering a Thud strike on the Thai Nguyen steel mills. Bill Kirk was on the wing, with Dick Pascoe and Norm Wells as the second element. After the strike, the flight came back up Thud Ridge, covering the strike force egress. Bill Lafever again:

"We were below Thud Ridge, no SAMs, nobody was shooting at us, we had lots of gas. The Navy (with whom the strike had been co-ordinated) had gone home; the Thuds had gone home. Out to one side of us, was the fighter airfield at Phuc Yen, protected by wall-to-wall SAMs and AAA. And then I got four bogeys on the radar. And I said 'you got the dot.' And he said 'you know what they are?' And I said 'yes sir, they're MiGs.' And he says 'you know, we can go down, get one, maybe two, but to do that we'd have to drag this four ship across all that flak and all them SAMs.' So we turned around and went back home!"

Political restrictions reduced air activity over North Vietnam from early in 1968, the last USAF victory being scored in February of that year, although the USN engaged in desultory fighting until September. Air fighting effectively recommenced early in 1972, in which year two pilot and three backseater aces emerged. They were Randall Cunningham and William Driscoll of the US Navy, and Steve Ritchie, Charles DeBellevue and Geoffrey Feinstein of the USAF. Cunningham and Driscoll were a team for all their victories whereas Ritchie and DeBellevue scored four as a team and the remainder with other pilots, while Feinstein flew with no less than four different pilots for his five victories.

By an odd coincidence, Ritchie and DeBellevue scored their first victory earlier on the same day that Cunningham and Driscoll notched up an epic triple triumph which made them the first aces of the war. Of the two pilot aces, it is notable that all Cunningham's kills were scored with the Sidewinder, while all Ritchie's used the Sparrow. The combat circumstances also varied. The USAF, not to be outdone by the USN, were pushing Ritchie to get his five, giving him the lead on MIGCAP flights, whereas Cunningham's triple victory of May 10, 1972 was achieved while flying a flak suppression mission. Of one thing there can be little doubt; the Navy pair were involved in far more close combat and confused multi-bogey situations than the Air Force flyers.

Both the Navy and the Air Force had long been concerned that the victory/loss ratio achieved in Korea was not being repeated in Vietnam, but the Navy had actually started to do something about it, introducing air combat training using fighters of dissimilar characteristics as adversaries, a program later developed into the famous "Top Gun," and paralleled after the war by the USAF Aggressor program. During the early part of the war the Navy fighters had performed only marginally better than their Air Force counterparts in an arguably less exacting tactical scenario. During 1972, while the USAF victory/loss ratio stayed at just under 3:1, that of the USN leaped to over 8:1, an enormous increase. In common

with many Navy flyers, Cunningham had benefited greatly
from the combat training scheme, and put his newly acquired
skills to excellent use. Radar played little part in his engagements, but Driscoll in the back seat gave invaluable assistance
by visually checking the dangerous rear quadrant and calling
out threats, thereby giving Cunningham the all-round picture
and enabling him to concentrate on the task in hand.

Shortly after the war, Cunningham wrote a paper called
Air-to-Air Tactics. The opening paragraph is pure situational
awareness.

> "The key to success in air-to-air combat is the pilot, his
> ability, training, and aggressiveness, with a little luck
> thrown in. You cannot enter the air thinking that you will
> lose. Personality characteristics have to be oriented toward
> the mission, and concentration directed to maximum per-
> formance. There are no points for second place. The pilot
> must have a three-dimensional sense of awareness and feel
> time, distance and relative motion as if they were part of
> his soul; only if you have a feeling for what is going on
> around you can you take action and make correct deci-
> sions. Analyzing multiple complex time and space oriented
> problems correctly is one significant key to aerial combat."

Situational awareness had become a buzzword toward the
end of the war in South-East Asia. The above definition is the
best formulated up to this time, encompassing as it does, psy-
chology, training and instinct.

The Middle Eastern and South-East Asia conflicts had in
the main been fought with equipment that was quite elderly in
concept, albeit updated. The 1970s saw a whole new generation aircraft enter service, with higher thrust/weight ratios for
greater acceleration and climb, lower wing loadings for better
turning performance, and far more advanced electronics for
detection, self protection, and communications. Multi-mode
radars with a genuine look-down capability and the ability to
track multiple targets while continuing to search for more,
were combined with improved displays which filtered out un-
wanted mush via the computer and gave missile launch solu-
tions in the form of alpha-numeric information, projected onto

a head-up display focused at infinity, which enabled the pilot to keep looking out of the window as he jockeyed for position, rather than having to glance down into the cockpit. AEW aircraft now carried fighter controllers and became known as AWACS aircraft, able to detect and track the enemy at more than 200 miles range, projecting information directly onto the cockpit displays of the fighters via data link, thus cutting out the inevitable confusion caused by voice transmissions, which might be garbled, jammed, or simply blotted out by other transmissions made simultaneously. This greatly increased the SA of the pilot, while the data link information could be used to reduce that of the enemy, putting contacts onto the fighter displays without having to use its on-board radar, which could therefore be left on standby, for use when needed, minimizing the telltale emissions that would betray the fighter's presence to the foe.

In 1982 two further wars broke out, which could hardly have been more different in character. The South Atlantic War was fought around the Falkland Islands between Britain and Argentina, while Israel clashed with Syria in the skies of Lebanon. In the first of these, there is little of relevance to us, although the air fighting ended in a resounding victory for the Sea Harriers of the Royal Navy. Lacking airborne early warning, the Sea Harriers were forced to adopt the wasteful and inadequate system of standing patrols, while Argentina rarely sent fighters into the area to contest air superiority, most combats occurring when low flying attack aircraft were intercepted.

In complete contrast was the conflict between Israel and Syria over the Bekaa Valley, which ended in a claimed score of 85 to nil in favor of the Israelis. The Syrian Air Force was numerous and well equipped, mainly with MiG-21s and -23s in the fighter role, plus Sukhoi Su-17s and -22s for ground attack. The Israelis fielded Kfirs, Phantoms and Skyhawks, plus the new generation F-15 Eagles and F-16 Fighting Falcons, backed up by the E-2C Hawkeye AEW aircraft.

Badly outnumbered in the air, the Israelis proceeded to load the dice. Their first move was to detect and map all the Syrian ground radars in the area, using mainly remotely piloted vehicles for the purpose. The RPVs were then used to bring the radars on line, when they were attacked with Shrike anti-radiation missiles and Maverick guided bombs, followed up with cluster bombs, and in some cases, artillery fire. The blinding of the Syrian detection systems was completed with wholesale jamming, both active and passive, ground-and air-based. Then when the Syrian Air Force reacted, they were flying blind, reliant solely on their on-board radars and avionics, which were also subject to heavy jamming. Not so the Israeli fighters which, controlled by the Hawkeyes, cut a deadly swathe through the Syrian ranks, whose SA had by this time been reduced to what the pilots could see visually, for all practical purposes, the Syrians reporting that their ground-to-air communications were also subjected to heavy jamming, as were their navigation systems.

Soviet Colonels Dubrov and Kislyakov, writing in *Aviatsiya i kosmonavtika* in 1984, noted some interesting points about the air fighting, especially as it concerned the two American-built superfighters in Israel service, the F-15 and F-16.

" . . . Sparrow medium-ranged missiles were employed by Israeli F-15 fighters in approximately one third of all recorded attacks. The effectiveness was, however, acknowledged to be poor . . . Excessively lengthy tracking was at variance with the increased pace of combat . . . It was not possible to fire missiles at several targets at the same time. Therefore the bulk of the burden in air combat was assumed by the light F-16 fighters, which carried cannon and Sidewinders. Contrary to expectations, combat continued to be fought by maneuvering groups of aircraft at close quarters . . . The tactic based on a climbing attack from low level ambush (a dead zone in the Syrian radar coverage) was extensively employed. Mountain ranges, which created blind areas . . . helped conceal an F-15 in attack position. After reaching medium altitude, undetected closing was ensured by passive or active jamming originating from another aircraft . . ."

It was also noticeable that instead of operating in flights and elements, the F-15s tended to disperse beyond visual dis-

Slightly smaller than the Tomcat, and with but one crewman, the F-15 Eagle was designed solely for the air superiority role. While it carries a comprehensive electronics suite, it also has an unsurpassed view from the cockpit, there being virtually no blind spot astern, as can be seen here. (MCDONNELL DOUGLAS)

As in the early 1970s fighters got more capable, they also got larger
and more expensive, and therefore fewer. A reversal of the trend came
in the shape of the F-16; a small, agile, lightweight fighter optimized for
close combat. At close range, small is neat; it is more difficult to see.
(GENERAL DYNAMICS)

tance in order to create conditions favorable for the use of
their medium-range missiles. Although as the distance closed
they recombined into elements of two at least, which called
for a thoroughly well thought-out battle plan. At the merge,
F-16s formed the first echelon, while the larger and more expensive F-15 formed the second echelon.

Although the Israelis possessed a qualitative advantage
with which to oppose the quantitative advantage of the Syrians, it appears that they spared no effort to maximize their
edge, working very hard to ensure that the Syrian fighter
pilots were only aware of what they could see from their
cockpits, while they were shot at from beyond visual range by
the F-15s before being subjected to carefully co-ordinated at-

tacks by both F-16s and F-15s. The final scoreline confirms the effectiveness of these tactics, which reduced the Syrians to impotence. The figures released vary, and do not tally with the claimed total of victories, but it seems likely that both the F-15 and F-16 accounted for about forty aircraft each; while Kfirs claimed three, and a solitary MiG fell to a Phantom.

Epilogue

Technology has brought with it great advances, but also great penalties. The modern jet fighter is a far more lethal machine than its stick and string forebears, both to its opponents and to its pilot should he make an error of judgement. During the First World War, aircraft were cheap and quick to build, and flying training, such as it was, was of short duration. Set against the blood and waste of the trenches, a high level of fatal accidents during non-combat flights was acceptable; it was just a drop in the bucket. In the Second World War, aircraft were a bit more complex and rather more expensive, while flying training took longer, but much the same attitude prevailed; that it was impossible to make an omelet without breaking a few eggs. Then in the fifteen years between 1945 and 1960, technology ran riot. High performance fighters, with expensive guided missiles and even more expensive avionics demanded a higher level of pilot training, which took longer and cost more, while the fact that these years were essentially ones of peace made high attrition levels unacceptable. The ambiguous situation arose that while theoretically training for war, the peacetime fighter pilot was one who flew his aircraft safely and well, without breaking either it or himself. As American Colonel "Boots" Boothby put it: "How do you train for the most dangerous game in the world by being as safe as possible? When you don't let a guy train because its dangerous, you're saying, 'Go fight those lions with your bare hands in that arena, because we can't teach you how to use a spear. If we do, you might cut your finger while you're learning.'" The case might be overstated, but the principle is correct.

This series of three pictures show what may well be the future both in fighter cockpit displays, and in electronic SA. It is the McDonnell Douglas "Big Picture" concept, on which presentations can be shown, with data superimposed if necessary. Instructions can be given to the system by a touch of a finger, or perhaps a light pen, or by the time this very sophisticated system is ready to enter service, by voice. On the other hand, it does seem that it would be very vulnerable to battle damage, or even a power failure. Star Wars was nothing like this! (MCDONNELL DOUGLAS)

As a direct result, the selection procedure for fast jet pilots became more picky, concentrating on flying and systems operation potential rather than fighting potential. The underlying idea was that if a young man could be taught to handle the machine well, he could also be taught to fight it. This principle was fine for peacetime, but it overlooked the need to sift out the candidate with exceptional wartime potential, in a nutshell, those with the ace factor, many of whom inevitably must have slipped the net. It is an interesting consideration that many First World War aces, and not a few of World War 2, would never have got a place in the cockpit of a modern jet

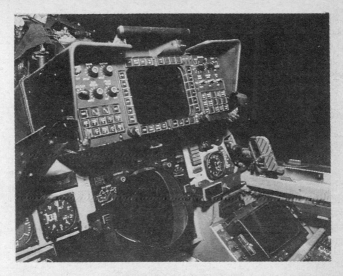

The combat is largely controlled from the back seat of the Tomcat, seen here. The digital display at top has a programmable keyboard to punch up the information needed. Below it is the circular tactical information display, which can show up to twelve potential targets, while the radar tracks and keeps a file on a further twelve. Information can also be accepted from outside sources such as AEW aircraft, via data link. The TID can be changed at will from having the Tomcat located at the bottom of the screen, and displaying what is out front, to placing the Tomcat at the center, in which case hostile aircraft working their way around for a stern attack, can also be seen coming. The tracks displayed are allocated by computer on a priority basis, which can be over-ridden at need by the operator. Information is presented in a filtered, clutter-free alpha-numeric format. (HUGHES)

fighter. Mannock and Galland had defective vision in one eye; while Ira Jones had faulty depth perception, as his record of wrecking over twenty aircraft on landing testifies. Boelcke tended to be asthmatic, while the frail Guynemer would never have been allowed through the airfield gates. Slow learners, such as Ball and Stanford Tuck, would almost certainly have been washed out during initial flying training, while what chance would Douglas Bader have had? Yet how much poorer would the history of air combat have been without these men. It is a moot point whether if SA could be definitely identified and quantified, that both physical and educational requirements should be relaxed in certain cases to take account of it.

Fighter development over the past four decades can be seen as a response to a threat, the major protagonists being the countries of NATO on the one hand and those of the Warsaw Pact on the other. At the outset, the West held a decided technological lead, which the East countered with numerical strength. Had a major clash occurred, the West would have been forced to reply on quality; the East on quantity. The outcome of any such clash is of course pure speculation, but Saber Measures (Charlie) appeared, as we saw in Chapter 1, in a protracted conflict, to favor the big battalions. There is also little doubt that in air combat, the confusion factor rises

The cockpit of the Mirage 2000C shows almost no traditional dials and gauges, these having been replaced by CRT displays with warning lights to indicate when something is amiss, on which details can be called up onto one or other of the screens. (AMD-BA/AVIAPLANS)

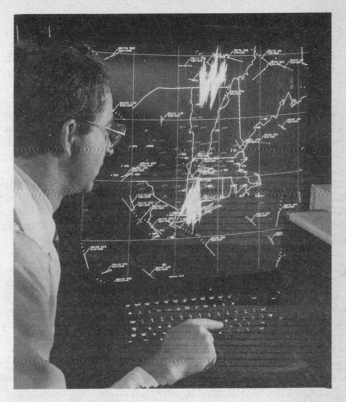

The Battle of Britain Ops Room table display seen earlier has long since been replaced by more modern, automated kit. We can imagine it to look something rather like this in the broad picture, broken down into smaller areas for local operational control. (HUGHES)

sharply in relation to the number of participants, and that confusion tends to degrade technology, particularly in the electronic arena.

Faced with an insurmountable numerical imbalance, the West started to chase its own tail. Fighters were made ever more capable, firstly with improved performance, secondly with more deadly armament, and thirdly with more clever avionic systems; the fighter actually became a weapons system. It also became larger, and vastly more expensive, which meant that less could be afforded in terms of both purchase and running costs. By 1972, the USAF Tactical Air Command had shrunk to about a third of the size that it had been twenty years earlier. The Soviet Union also had the same sort of problems, but to a lesser degree, as in general their kit was simpler. The inevitable result was that the available forces in the West shrank and the numerical imbalance grew, so that better fighters were needed to offset greater numbers, which were again more expensive, and so on. It finally reached the stage where the two American superfighters, the F-14 and F-15, were so expensive that they became counterproductive, a factor that led to the development of the smaller and cheaper F-16 and F/A-18 to pad out the numbers, which would otherwise have dropped to unacceptable levels.

What all this overlooked was that the dominant factor in air fighting has always been pilot quality. The selection process was, of course, based on pilot quality, and their training was of the best, but it was peacetime pilot quality and peacetime training. In the event of war, the peacetime pilot was to become an ace via clever electronics and wonder missiles. This situation was rather analogous to that of the hardware. Fighters were being built which were of excellent quality, and meant to last for twenty years or more. In a war situation an operational life of twenty months would be very good, and depending on the intensity of the fighting, twenty days might prove to be a fair average life. The fighters were being built for peacetime use; not for war, and the pilots followed the same pattern. The Soviet Union adopts a much more pragmatic view of these things. Take as an example their jet engines; they are designed for a life between major overhauls which is little longer than the time that they expect them to last in combat, and which is far less than their Western counterparts. As for training, they know and accept that people occasionally get killed; they try to minimize it, but not at the expense of realism.

The really sophisticated AEW systems are far beyond the purse of most countries, although the value of AEW is undisputed. But any AEW is better than none, and this is the display of the Skymaster AEW radar as installed in the Defender airframe. Although limited by comparison with the big boys, it still represents a large increment in pilot SA. (THORN EMI)

The Bekaa Valley fighting in 1982 demonstrated conclusively what could be achieved by quality against quantity, and an 85 to nil kill ratio is impressive by any standards. On the other hand, we should be careful not to read the wrong lessons into it. Certainly the Israelis, with their F-15s and F-16s, had superior fighters, and equally certainly their pilot quality was

The modern fighter cockpit, with two CRT displays plus the Hud, the desired information being called up by pushbutton. This small but comfortable cockpit belongs to the Tigershark. (NORTHROP)

better than that of their opponents, whom the Israelis admitted appeared to operate without regard for basic tactical considerations. But the truth is almost certainly that the difference lay in the situational awareness of the opposing pilots; the Israelis knowing where the Syrian flyers were and what they were doing, while the comm-jammed and radar-jammed Syrians

Flexible air defense need not be a costly item. This data link terminal can be mounted in the back of a Land Rover and not only displays message and target information received from AEW aircraft, but can pass the data into the GCI network. (THORN EMI)

knew only what they could see out of the window, which in most cases was not a lot. There can be no guarantee that in any further conflict that the same degree of SA can be attained, and in the "worst case" scenario of a major war in Central Europe, it certainly will not be.

Down the years, the fighter pilot has gradually had more and more information to assimilate. Initially it was little more than what his view from the cockpit could tell him. With the introduction of radio and ground control, this was expanded into what was in the area, the direction it was going and the height it was at, although the information was rarely either accurate or complete. As operational speeds and altitudes in-

Work is already advanced to allow pilots to give and receive information to and from their aircraft by voice, to reduce the workload on every other interactive part of their body. Part of this will obviously take the form of an electronic wingman guarding the tail, while the pilot can tell the aircraft when to shoot. All will be well unless the pilot emulates Marshall Murat's error at the battle of Borodino, when he confused the instruction "scheusse" with "scheisse"! This is the TI voice interactive system. (TEXAS INSTRUMENTS)

creased, accurate navigation assumed greater importance than before. The advent of homing missiles expanded the volume of sky around him from which he was vulnerable, while on-board radar helped him search beyond visual range but was yet something else to watch. Fuel calculations became ever more critical, while radar warning receivers of ever-increasing complexity, combined with the integrated air defense system of radar-laid guns, SAMs and fighters all increased in workload. "Switchology" became a new buzzword. The pilot had to handle navigation and attack systems, make weapons selections, alter radar modes as necessary, communicate with both other aircraft and the ground, and operate countermeasures systems. In his spare time, he flew the aircraft and chewed gum, although not both together. As avionic systems grew increasingly clever, so he was subjected to a veritable information explosion, often more than he could comfortably handle. F-15 driver Dito Ladd once likened it to trying to get a drink from a fire hose.

Now while all this information was important, an increasing amount of the pilot's time was spent in trying to assimilate it. To keep the workload within manageable limits, flying and maneuvering the fighter had to become second nature. USAF Aggressor training is very demanding in this sphere, because the Aggressor pilots fly the lightweight and simple F-5E, frequently against the world-beating Tomcat, Eagle, and Fighting Falcon, against which it is totally outclassed in terms of basic hardware. The Aggressor is taught to know what his machine is doing purely by feel. For example, at one point he flies a 5g turn watching the instruments. He then performs the same maneuver looking forward, without using instruments. Finally, he has to pull a 5g turn while looking back over his

Fighter avionics design is about achieving pilot SA, but the EF-111A Raven shown here is a tactical jamming system dedicated to spoiling enemy SA. The "Electric Fox," as it is commonly known, is a Grumman conversion of the F-111 bomber. (GRUMMAN)

right shoulder, with his left hand on the stick. Only when he can consistently reproduce a 5g turn under these conditions to within half a g either way, is he allowed to progress to the next phase. Unloaded acceleration is another exercise that must be mastered. The time taken to accelerate from one set speed to another must be done by feel, again while scanning the sky astern.

Oswald Boelcke made the first faltering steps towards comparing the performance of different aircraft and finding the areas where his own machine had an advantage. Over the years this was honed to a fine edge, mainly by means of empirical trials. While this was not very satisfactory, it was better than nothing. Then in the 1960s, Major John Boyd of the USAF, formulated the concept of energy maneuverability. It is obvious that an aircraft needs energy in order to climb and to accelerate. It is perhaps less obvious that it needs more energy to turn than to fly straight and level. In flight, every aircraft has what is known as an energy state, which is made up of

The Grumman EA-6 Prowler is a dedicated electronic warfare aircraft which carries a massive battery of jammers which are operated by a four-man crew. Its purpose is to render enemy aircraft solely reliant on what they can see with their eyes from the cockpit. It can also perform triangulation functions to locate the source of hostile jamming, and pass attack data to the waiting Tomcats. (GRUMMAN)

Technical advances have resulted in very capable radars being pack-aged into a small space. This is the multi-mode APG-65 carried by the F/A-18 Hornet. (HUGHES)

two things. Positional energy is composed of the weight of the airplane times its altitude, while kinetic energy is its dynamic motion, expressed as half velocity squared times mass. The sum of these two is in total energy, and represents the theoretical altitude which could be attained if all the energy was converted into height. The energy state determines the maneuver capability of the airplane at any given moment. Of course, the engine is pumping more energy into the fighter each second, but this is often depleted faster than it can be replaced. In close combat, it is not only necessary to know the strengths and limitations of one's own machine at any given moment, but to recognize those of the adversary, via his energy state. This is an important part of SA; knowing when the enemy can be out-turned or when he has the advantage. As the old saying goes, "out of altitude, airspeed and ideas." A fighter allowed to become low and slow is virtually defenseless; it cannot dive to pick up speed, and it can barely turn. Energy charts can be calculated for any type of aircraft and comparisons made between types. The well-trained pilot will, in combat, know pretty well exactly where he can out-turn his opponent, or where he can out-climb or out-accelerate him, and also where the converse is true, and modify his tactics accordingly. For close fighting, he will also have a bag of tricks called basic fighter maneuvers, from which he will select one appropriate to the situation in hand, and hope that it works as well as it did in practice.

All this the pilot must know and be able to handle unerringly, as well as handling complicated switch functions. It is little wonder that at times the workload gets too high and he is max'ed out, but even then, some perform better than others. The aim, through constant training and practice, is for the pilot to achieve a high level of proficiency. This is analogous to professional sportsmen, particularly in the area of team ball games. Like air combat, just a few of them are outstanding in their chosen sport, the aces perhaps. No one knows what really makes them stand out against their fellows; it is equally certain that they have spells of being off-form, but basically they have flair. Others train and practice just as hard, but cannot obtain the same results, except perhaps on rare occa-

Small fighters may have advantages in close combat, but they are also vulnerable to their larger and more capable brethren at BVR distances. While it is possible to hang big missiles and a compatible radar on a small airframe, it is, as defense systems analyst Pierre Sprey once said, like hanging an anchor on the airplane! This is graphically illustrated by this picture of the F-20 Tigershark launching an AIM-7F Sparrow. (NORTHROP)

Situational awareness has been brought to new levels by this team; two Tomcats and an E-2C Hawkeye from the same stable. All three aircraft have systems which can "talk" to each other via data link, and also to other aircraft similarly fitted, and to the control ship. They would also be further assisted by an EA-6B Prowler electronic warfare aircraft, also a Grumman product, the function of which is to jam enemy emissions and assist in interception problems.(GRUMMAN)

sions. But no matter how hard the fighter pilot trains, there remains that indefinable something which makes the difference between being an ace and being merely good.

Oddly enough, the technological quest to make each "good" flyer an ace through weapons lethality, was to turn up the best clue yet to the ace factor. As part of the testing of the next generation of launch and leave missiles, a very extensive program, featuring both radar and communications jamming against a realistic defensive and offensive scenario, was run through a "twin-tub" air combat similator. The fighters used both the projected missile and a baseline one that was already in service, and many hundreds of multi-bogey combats were simulated. Many current pilots, of varied experience levels, took part in the program. It was naturally expected that the new magic missile would make a considerable difference, and of course, it did. But another factor entered the equation. A few pilots were found to be almost invariably successful, regardless of which weapons they were using, and regardless of scenario. A check was run to discover whether this could be due to experience levels, as one would expect that the experienced pilots would be better than relative novices. It was found that there was no relationship between experience and success. This was a turnup for the book, and other possibilities were checked, again with no conclusive results. Then it was suggested that the results were checked with SA, rather reluctantly one imagines, as SA was still ill-defined and un-quantifiable, only one stage removed from witchcraft, and definitely subjective rather than objective.

The first step was to find a means of quantifying SA. This was done subjectively by the pilots themselves, and the test observers, working as a team. The observers attended the "pre-flight" briefing, then watched the encounter as it developed, assessing each individual pilot. A further assessment was made at the debrief, at which each pilot gave his own assessment. Then the engagement was repeated on a large screen, so that all could see exactly what had happened, after which the pilots would re-assess themselves. Finally both observers and pilots would mutually debrief and assess SA on an agreed points system. Hardly scientific, it was the best that could be done. After many test simulations, the findings were compared. The result was almost 100 percent positive. For individual engagements, the pilots with the best kill ratio (in a multi-bogey, degraded electronics environment, it should be remembered) had the highest SA scores. Even further, some pilots were found to have better kill ratios consistently, and these were those with the highest SA ratings.

From this it seems that SA *is* the ace factor, and not only

The greatest modern aid to SA is the Boeing E-3A Sentry AWACS aircraft, capable of keeping track of over 200 aircraft within a radius of roughly 240 nautical miles. This is how it will appear in French service. (BOEING)

can it be identified, but it can be approximately quantified also. If this is so, it seems that a great improvement in force effectiveness can be achieved by careful selection procedures. There is just one doubt. Simulation, like air combat training, is a sterile environment. Good simulation never killed anyone yet, to misquote Mannock. Simulators, like training flights, are an invitation to be fancy, with supper on the table at home even if it goes wrong. When real missiles are flying, the temptation is strongly resisted. As USN Phantom veteran Robert Shaw has commented, "in combat, anything more than a level turn feels exotic." It is also widely known that the US Navy aviators, trained to use the "loose deuce" style of flying, where both aircraft in the element carry out sequenced attacks, commonly reverted to the leader/wingman in Vietnam, when the shooting was for real. Therefore there was an element of unreality in the trials, and the vital question of how the pilots would have fared in real life, remains unanswered. The trials referred to took place many years ago, and if any further progress has been made, it has been kept under wraps.

A further hindrance to progress is that a fighter force needs X number of pilots as a baseline force size, below which it will be unable to carry out its assigned tasks. The West relies on volunteers, and there are barely enough of the required quality, so perhaps there is little point in going further. On the other hand, the pilots with high SA should be identified, and groomed as future flight and squadron commanders, where they will have a greater effect in any future conflict than they would have as individuals.

The present trend is still to use technology as the ace factor by increasing the situational awareness of the pilots using electronic means, and providing them with ever more lethal missiles. To date, reliable identification has bedevilled beyond visual range combat. Jtids (Joint Tactical Information and Distribution System) should cure this once and for all, by positively identifying all aircraft within its detection orbit as friend or foe, then transmitting the information directly onto the screens of the fighters via secure data link. The fighters will thereby be enabled to enter the arena in electronic silence, with radars on standby.

Stealth features will also be widely used for fighters of the future, thus reducing enemy SA. The pilot workload will remain high, but the two-seater fighter, in which the load is shared, seems to have halted with the dedicated interceptors, such as the F-14 Tomcat, Tornado F3, and the MiG-31 Foxhound. While a two-man crew can work very effectively as a team, it seems to be felt that the need for them to communicate with each other is a hindrance in the air superiority mission, although not when flying a fairly autonomous mission as an interceptor. Of course, misunderstandings are possible. This has always been a feature of two-seaters, as an incident in 1916 shows.

An FE 2d of No. 25 Squadron, RFC, flown by Sergeant Walder, with Captain Baynes as observer, shot down a German aircraft after a brief encounter. As the German went down, Baynes turned to Walder and shouted above the engine noise "shot up arse." Walder agreed, smiling and nodding, only to get the angry blast of "not them, ME!" from Baynes, who had taken a German bullet in his bum.

The current trend in air superiority fighters is the single-seater, and various schemes are in hand to ease the pilot's workload. His hands and eyes are too busy already, as are his

Electro-optics can give great advantages in combat. Here an F-14 is seen on the television camera system of another Tomcat, at ten times the normal visual range. (NORTHROP)

ears, while his feet are limited in what they can do. In the fighter of the future, and perhaps some extant today, he will be able to ask the onboard computer to perform certain functions, and it will comply. The main difficulty in this field is speech recognition, with regional accents or hoarseness a major problem to be overcome. Voice warnings of critical flight states have been around for many years.

The next proposed advance is in the cockpit displays. The cockpit is, to use the current jargon, the man/machine interface. Most of the instrument panel, and the consoles on each side are taken up with knobs and switches, dial and tape instruments, with one or more cathode ray tube screens. All of these have a necessary function, but they take up a lot of space, and apart from the CRT displays, have no flexibility. The F/A-18 Hornet is currently regarded as the nearest thing to a man/machine symbiosis, with three CRT displays which can flash up information on a variety of things at the press of a button. This still leaves the pilot with three screens, plus many instruments to monitor. A further restriction is the head-up display, which is unavoidably small and narrow. At most, a quarter of the instrument panel can present information about the tactical situation, and even this required the dexterity of a concert pianist to call up effectively, while weapons aiming demands that the target be visible through the small Hud area.

Then, in October 1986, McDonnell Douglas unveiled a new concept in cockpit displays which is intended to present virtually all the information a pilot needs in a tactical combat situation. All the information available from the on-board sensors and external sources is to be gathered together in the "Big Picture" concept, which is in essence a CRT display filling the entire area of the instrument panel. In addition to air threats, located ground threats, identified and with their weapons envelope projected, will be shown. As Gene Adam of McDonnell Douglas stated, ". . . the numerical superiority, complexity and sophistication of tomorrow's threats will be too much for the displays and dials common to today's cockpits . . . It will reduce the pilot's workload, but more importantly, 'Big Picture' increases the pilot's situational awareness so that during each phase of a mission the pilot has one source of information about the target, enemy air and ground threats, friendly forces and their relationship to the intended mission profile, and the status of his weapons. The result: a more efficient interface between man and machine."

Most of the technology exists for Big Picture, and there is no reason to believe that both the hardware and the software could not reach the flight development stage in five years or so. It is further planned to operate Big Picture in conjunction with a helmet-mounted display under development by Kaiser Electronics which would both present the close combat tactical situation, and allow off-boresight weapons aiming.

There can be no doubt that technology can vastly increase

The fighter that has everything. The F-14A Tomcat is a weapons system in the truest sense of the word. Not only does it have a very long ranged radar and an excellent threat warning system, but it was the first of the breed of Mach 2-capable fighters to give its crew good all-around cockpit visibility. (GRUMMAN)

both a pilot's survival capability and his lethality. Fighter fly-by-wire control systems have already demonstrated what is possible by translating the pilot's inputs into the limit of what is possible within the bounds of the flight envelope. The F-16, affectionately referred to as the "Electric Jet" has the reputation of making all pilots good, because it does most of the work for them, giving so-called carefree handling. On the other hand, it does not make them aces. An exercise in 1984 saw Danish F-16 drivers arriving at the merge with no tally and no visual contact, a condition hardly likely to please their insurers. However good the aircraft, and however fantastic the systems and lethal the weapons, a handful of pilots will still emerge as exceptional in the air combat arena. They will be the ones with the mysterious ability to extract, retain, and project more from the available information than their fellows. They will be the ones with the ace factor.

Appendix

No Guts—No Glory

By: Major General Frederick C. Blesse

Objectives of Tactical Formation

Tactical Formation is employed to achieve the following broad objectives:

1. To achieve maximum maneuverability for offensive air-to-air operations (Offensive Tactical Formation).
2. To achieve maximum mutual support and visual cross-over for defensive air-to-air operation (Defensive Tactical Formation).
3. To assign definite responsibilities to each member of the flight and provide a chain of consecutive command authority in order to maintain unity within the flight throughout the mission regardless of any unforeseen difficulties.
4. To enable each member of the flight to perform cruise control consistent with the requirements of the mission and to accomplish his own navigation in addition to fulfilling the duties required from all members of an effective combat team.

Practically all Tactical Formations are a compromise between maximum maneuverability and maximum mutual support, and the extent of the compromise depends upon the requirements of the mission to be flown. Since we shall always be on the offensive unless forced to be otherwise, let us first consider the Offensive Tactical Formation.

Offensive Tactical Formation

Let us start with the most elementary of the basic problems—the position of the wingman on a typical mission where enemy fighter opposition is expected. What is it we want from the wingman? We want him to do two things: (1) fly his aircraft in such a way that regardless of the leader's maneuvers, he will not become separated and (2) look around. If item (1) is not put first in his duties, he obviously will not perform his primary purpose in being there, that of supplying the eyes to the rear of the lead aircraft. We see then that, unless the wingman can get flexibility and maneuverability, in the position he flies, he is in constant danger of being separated, especially when the element or flight is attacking or under attack. He must be able to look around. Through experience in Korea, we found the position best adapted to meet these two important requirements was:

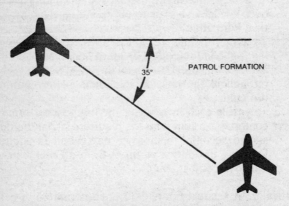

PATROL FORMATION

35°

THE DISTANCE BETWEEN AIRCRAFT IS SUCH THAT THE WINGMAN CAN JUST BARELY READ THE LARGE NUMBERS ON THE FUSELAGE OF THE LEADER'S AIRCRAFT.

Patrol formation in MiG Alley. Spacing was such that the wingman could just read the large numbers on his leader's fuselage.

1. For patrolling, have the wingman fly about 35 degrees back and out only as far as he can still read the large numbers on the side of his leader's aircraft. This is as far forward and as far out as the wingman should ever get unless lack of fuel or some other circumstance renders the element useless offensively.

2. When enemy aircraft are sighted, the wingman moves into a *fighting* position. (He does not move in along the 35 degree angle line, but along a line perpendicular to the flight path of his leader's aircraft.)

In the fighting position, the wingman will probably be able to read the small numbers on the vertical stabilizer and will be back from his leader about 55 degrees. These are only crutches for the beginner to use. He actually flies, not in a position, but in an area—cutting off, crossing, sliding to trail,

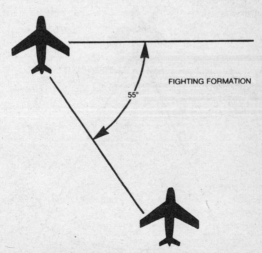

FIGHTING FORMATION

55°

THE DISTANCE BETWEEN AIRCRAFT IS SUCH THAT THE WINGMAN CAN PLAINLY READ THE SMALL NUMBERS ON THE VERTICAL STABILIZER OF THE LEADER'S AIRCRAFT

Fighting formation in MiG Alley. The aircraft spacing was such that the wingman could read the small numbers on his leader's tail.

doing what's necessary to stay with his leader. Now it only takes a moment for one to realize that this is pretty close to the leader, but that is what is needed to an aerial fight. The wingman must be close enough to his leader to make it necessary for an enemy aircraft to actually out-perform and out-maneuver the leader himself in order to shoot down the wingman. Just one ride in this proper position will be a little discouraging to the average pilot for, during the early state of training, not much time can be spared for looking around.

A few tips for the wingman now before we leave this subject. Consider your fuselage in relation to your leader's fuselage when maintaining position. Keep your fuselage stacked just slightly down at all times on your leader. When turned into, resist the temptation to drop way down with your wings in the same plane as your leader. Drop down a few feet, per-

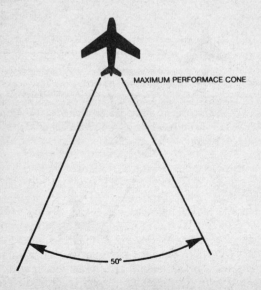

MAXIMUM PERFORMACE CONE

50°

The maximum performance cone for the wingman lay in about 25 degrees to either side of this leader's centerline.

haps, but then hold what you have and see what happens. If you have trouble seeing the leader, or if you begin creeping forward (as you may when he tightens up his turn), ease off your bank and slide toward the trail position. Since you have no idea (and neither does the leader, actually) just how far around the leader is going, stay five or six ship lengths from him in trail, if necessary, and hang on 'til he eases off on the Gs. At low altitudes, stay on the inside of the turn whenever possible. Cross or slide toward trail position when G forces make it necessary—but, *not until*. Remember this: You'll know when it's time to go to trail because you can't go anywhere else. There will be too many Gs and no visibility on the inside of the turn, and you will immediately be left behind on the outside. That only leaves this "Maximum performance cone" to which to slide.

During the initial encounter when the leader is maneuvering with an aggressive enemy pilot, it will be difficult for the wingman to do anything but hang on. During the maximum performance stage, as was stated above, hang on until the leader is no longer pulling maximum Gs, then immediately get to the inside of the turn and begin looking around again. Tell the leader what you see every time you are able to take a look. If you should become separated from your leader, give him a call immediately after being separated. If you are unsure of your location, tell him that immediately. Head for the pre-arranged rendezvous point, keeping Mach high and clearing yourself constantly.

High Altitude Formation Flying

High altitude means that altitude where you are beginning to lose the effect of your thrust and turning ability to the extent that maneuverability becomes a problem to you. Down low, your throttle gives you quick reaction; at high altitudes, however, you will be left behind after your leader rolls out of a turn that is into you. For this reason, a little different technique is required when flying at very high altitudes. As you increase altitude, the common conception is that you must spread further out. Nothing could be further from the truth. The higher you go, the less effect your thrust has on the aircraft; thus the time to move from one relative position on your leader to another is greatly increased. If it takes longer to get from patrol position to the fighting position at altitude, then the logical answer certainly is not to move further out and exaggerate your problem. Actually, the same formation you have used at lower altitudes will hold you in good stead, but even then your time to get to a fighting position will be increased. To cut this down you would have to go so close to your leader that you would spend too much time actually flying formation. Besides this, you can afford this extra little time required because your attacker will be longer in his curve of pursuit or attack; his performance is cut also.

Some things then that will help the wingman maintain his position on his leader are:

1. Use about the same distance from your leader that you did at low altitude.
2. As a wingman, do not attempt to stay on the inside of the turn the way you did at low altitudes. Concentrate on keeping your airspeed the same as your leader's. This means:
3. When turned into, ease across from inside to outside behind your leader. Change gradually as you gain. Once on the outside, slowly change sides again as he pulls away from you.
4. As an element leader using fluid element, gain a little altitude as you are turned into and rarely get more than a hair to the outside of the turn. As the turn is completed, drop on down to your normal position, trading the altitude you have gained for speed.
5. As a wingman, make all your stick movements gentle pressures or you will lose valuable airspeed by buffeting or stalling the aircraft.
6. As a flight leader, make gentle turns with your flight to preserve the Mach you have.
7. Watch tailpipe temperature; it increases quickly and will even go above limits at extreme altitudes and decreased Machs.

8. Use your oxygen system properly and get to lower altitudes if you have any reasons to suspect trouble.

9. Be more attentive to keeping your approximate position while you are flying wing. Once you get out of position at high altitude, it's going to take you a long time to get back.

10. Cruising at high Mach is imperative for high altitude work. A low airspeed at low altitude is a bad practice but at least the aircraft will still turn and maneuver. This is not true at high altitude.

11. The percentage of kills per sighting will drop off at high altitudes. Everything is too critical—no room for misjudgment.

Flight Leaders

1. BEFORE TAKE-OFF: Be certain every man knows his job before he gets in his aircraft. Make your briefings thorough. Brief so you cannot be misunderstood.

2. CLIMB OUT: If there is any possibility of meeting other aircraft during climb out, climb at higher than Tech Order airspeeds. Increase your climbing Mach as altitude increases. If you are climbing straight out, the element leader should be looking into the sun and the number 2 and number 4 men would naturally be on the outside of the formation. During climb out, ease your power up and try to get some idea about the speed of all the aircraft in your flight. As you increase power, note the percent at which the slowest first begins dropping behind and then give him about two percent to play with for the rest of the mission. You'll find having him with you when the fight starts will more than make up for the two percent of the power.

3. CRUISE:
   a. Cruise at a high Mach and you'll find you have an advantage on most enemy aircraft engaged.
   b. Steep turns when you are merely patrolling, only force the members of your flight to use excessive

power after a new course has been established. During a good, smooth, gentle turn, airspeeds will stay up and flight members can look around.

c. Find the con level. When possible, cruise with your high element just below con level and you'll quickly see any attack made on your flight from above.

4. COMBAT:

a. If your Mach is high when you sight the enemy, you will be in pretty fair shape.

b. Always turn to meet the attack whether you are element leader or flight leader. If you are an element leader, let your leader know where you are and what you are doing. While you are turning into him, trade your airspeed for altitude. This will shorten your radius of turn, allowing you to get further around toward the six o'clock position on the enemy. The altitude may also be useful depending on what the enemy does with his aircraft. Never use speed brakes during the initial maneuvering phase unless you have worked your way at least to the four or five o'clock position. Keep your eyes open and occasionally remind your wingman to look around.

c. Always designate a rendezvous point. If your wingman should become separated from you, stop fighting and get back together. Find out immediately what kind of shape he is in and if he knows his direction home or to the rendezvous point. He should be briefed to proceed to the rendezvous point at high Mach. Get your element together and get back into the fight. In combat as a single, it's generally best to keep your Mach up as high as possible and leave the area completely (clearing your tail every ten to fifteen seconds as you do so).

d. Generally when you slow down to maneuver with an aircraft, have your element high and fast to give you top cover. This is especially true in combat around airfields where landing enemy aircraft usually have a CAP flight airborne to fight off attackers.

e. Make sure that your wingmen look around. As the leader your eyes will have to be out in front of the flight looking for something to attack about eighty percent of the time. You must be able to depend on your wingmen to do most of the defensive looking.

f. Keep the aircraft you are attacking in sight. Once you spot him, you can't take your eyes from him for one second or you'll come back as one of the many who had him cold and let him slip away.

g. When attacking, *never* get in between the leader and his number two man. Cutting in between the leader and his wingman is the most inexcusable error a leader can make and one that cannot be condoned.

h. Check fuel carefully and often during the encounter. Inexperienced pilots and combat-wise pilots alike are very often forgetful when dog fighting and it's up to the leader to assemble the flight and bring it home so as to hit initial with ample fuel remaining in the lowest aircraft.

i. Try to operate your flight just as you would in combat, never forgetting, however, that you can only fly on the par with the weakest man in the flight.

j. In training, you must avoid these flight leader versus flight leader duels. You are not in front to impress anybody. You are out there to teach them. If you should get a man behind you, avoid "pride maneuvers." Pulling the aircraft straight up and then kicking it off into a semi-spin, or dropping gear or flaps, and other such senseless maneuvers would all get you shot down instantly in combat. There is also a good possibility of spinning a pilot of lesser ability into the ground.

Combat Tactics

No one can tell another what to do in a *future* air-to-air fight. We can only relate what we have done that worked effectively a good percentage of the time in the past, and hope that these basic sets of circumstances aid by forming a general background of knowledge from which you can draw instinctively when the chips are down. In this game, there is a great demand for the individual who can "play by ear."

Offensive Tactics

In the following cases, let us assume we can attack, ie, have airspeed or altitude and are the aggressors.

1. ONE ATTACKING TWO: Ordinarily, you don't stay around without a wingman, but you can always expect the unusual in combat. You may be a single on your next mission. A single aircraft with a pilot who is aggressive and well trained can tear a two or four ship flight to shreds unless every man in the four-ship knows his job backward and forward—a thing rarely seen. When attacking two aircraft, determine the feasibility of dropping unseen below them and gradually slipping into firing range from low and behind. Assuming this is impossible, begin a normal pass from any angle possible and note closely your overtaking speed. If the two aircraft stay together, drive on in using speed brakes around 2,000 ft. range to cut closing speed to where you can expect to fire a reasonable burst. If they break into you, turn with them as long as possible. If you begin to overshoot, slide high and to the rear still using speed brakes to cut speed. Then, depending on your desires, slide back down at six o'clock or stay high and reconsider. You must decide on the way in, whether you are going to slow down and attempt to get at six o'clock at their airspeed or just bounce and pull up. How well they are flying, how many enemy aircraft have been sighted in the area, whether you could be picked up if you had to bale out, how much fuel you have in case you make a mistake and have to hit the deck, are just a few of the major considerations before making this decision.

If you slow down, you may get both of them. If you YO YO, you stand a good chance of getting only a few sporadic hits. If you slow down and stay, get the wingman first. If you hit him or for any reason he breaks off, leaving his leader, watch him but let him go and switch to get the leader. The wingman probably will be too excited, especially if he is hit, to think of mutual support and the leader will be easy to get since you are already at six o'clock to him. After you nail the leader, then look again for the crippled wingman. Get him too if you can. If not, get out, keeping your airspeed up. The method of defense and your actions will usually follow a similar pattern. Remember, if properly trained, the one left free will turn back into you so take one and follow him as long as possible; then, at the last moment, change. Many times the supposedly attacked will commit himself to evasive maneuvers too early, leaving the other one a perfect, unprotected target. If this happens, you are fortunate. Let's see what happens if you aren't so fortunate.

As you commit yourself to one, he begins a turn into you, possibly a diving spiral immediately; this generally is a turn away from the other aircraft. Begin the turn with him, but watch the other aircraft carefully just as you did before. If he turns toward you and has timed it properly, he will drop in range behind you. Your only move then is to reverse into him to meet his attack. This can easily end in a scissors maneuver if he is a good, aggressive pilot, so be alert for a possible decrease of throttle and use of speed brakes. He may go right on by, since he has accomplished his purpose of making you leave his partner alone, in which case another reversal to chase him will put you to the rear of both aircraft once again. Now, press your attack on the most likely of the two, for they will probably be separated. Before you fire at one, look behind you for the other.

2. ONE ATTACKING FOUR: Note carefully the position of the second element. Whether they are high or low, attack the second element first. Keep your airspeed up as you close, for you can be sure when he turns into you, his turn will be away from the other element if he can arrange it. Your best chance, therefore, if the element is on the right of the leader, is to attack from the left side. If the element is on the left, attack from the right. This makes it necessary for the second element to break toward the lead element. This will increase your

chances for success, for it makes it more difficult for the leader to see what is going on when you are all directly behind and above him. Also, it brings the two elements closer together during the initial phase of your attack, which means you can delay a little longer before committing yourself completely to one element and force them into a defensive maneuver.

When they are out of mutual support position, shift your attack to the lead element and press this attack to the hilt, just as is indicated in the previous discussion of one aircraft attacking two. Look around. After a turn or two, the second element leader may work himself back to where he and his wingman can again help the lead element. If you overshoot, don't commit the foolhardy error of sliding level to the outside of the turn. When you can't hack the turn, trade airspeed for altitude and try to keep your aircraft behind his as you are pulling up.

3. TWO ATTACKING TWO: Look around carefully to make certain you are not attacking one of two elements. When you are sure you have really contacted a two-ship flight and not one element of a four-ship flight, begin your attack. You may be high, low, or level but regardless of what you have that enables you to attack, begin the maneuvering phase to put your two to the rear of the two you are attacking. If they don't see you, your job is simple. If they do see you, they will resist your effort to get behind them by a turn into you. This is the beginning of your dogfight.

If their turn is maximum performance, you probably will not be able to turn tight enough to continue closing and tracking at the same time. When you see you can't track, stop trying and either disengage or pull your nose up and to the rear of the two you are attacking. If the situation is such that you cannot slow down to their airspeed, then fire anytime you are in range and can track; if not, disengage by breaking down and away opposite their direction of turn. Disengage only if you are in imminent danger of being attacked by slowing down; otherwise, trade airspeed for altitude, keeping to their rear and using throttle and speed brakes as necessary to slide in at six o'clock.

Now watch yourself, for if the two are sharp, they will spread apart, causing you to again make an important decision. Your best move is to do one of two things: (a) Separate with them, each of you taking one aircraft; or (b) Stay together and attempt to make one pilot commit himself defensively to the point where he cannot help the other pilot. At this time, switch your attack and have the wingman watch carefully for the other enemy pilot.

4. TWO ATTACKING FOUR: Begin your attack on the second element and, if possible, from the lead element side. This will cause the element to break behind the leader and make mutual support more difficult between elements. It will bring the elements closer together also and allow you to switch your attack later in your initial pass. To be effective, you must make the second element believe you are really after them; believing this, they will be thinking very little of the lead

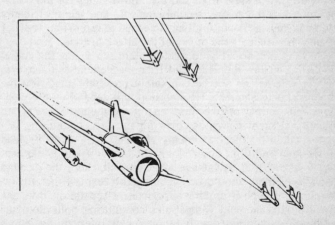

Two attacking four: as "BOOTS" Blesse said, make the second element believe you are really after them. As shown here, the two Sabres have forced the rear MiG element to break away, and are ideally placed to switch their attack to the lead element. To borrow a Soviet-style chess simile, this is rather like a discovered check, and is a classic example of deception, intended to destroy the enemy SA.

element. When you switch attacks at the last moment to the lead element, you will generally find the second element is no problem, having gone into a defensive spiral or some such maneuver and become separated from their lead element. If they should come back into you, turn into their attack and disengage before you become entangled with two to one offs and everyone at the same airspeed. If things go right, you'll be two behind two and can continue your attack as described in Number 3 above. But, look around!

5. FOUR ATTACKING FOUR: In a situation such as this, the lead friendly element should attack from the inside of the high enemy second element, or the enemy element farthest back. This is another of the many cases that must be played by ear. As the second enemy element breaks into the attack, they will probably go down as they can get help from the lead enemy element. The lead friendly element switches the attack, if possible, to the lead enemy element in which case the friendly second element stays high and fast and watches for the possible return of the enemy second element. The second friendly element stays as cover until he is needed to run off an attacker or until he becomes the object of the attack himself.

If it is not possible to switch elements when the initial bounce is made, then the lead friendly element will have to decide whether or not he can safely press his attack on the second enemy element. His decision will depend on the position and action of the first enemy element. The second friendly element serves as cover for the first, countering any action taken by the free enemy element. Any time the lead element (friendly) is attacked and the second friendly element has a substantial advantage over the attacker, the second friendly element should be encouraged to exploit this advantage even though it requires a permanent separation from the friendly lead element. Sometimes committing both elements to the offensive immediately by putting an interval of seven to ten seconds between attacking elements will be productive. The second element is frequently in a position to engage the enemy element attacked as it makes its initial defensive maneuver. By having both enemy elements engaged, you almost cut out the possibility of mutual support between enemy elements.

Basic Principles of Offense

1. The element of two aircraft is your most effective basic fighting team. When the fight is over, you will be coming home in twos about ninety percent of the time.
2. Two elements represent your most effective fighting unit—the flight.
3. If enemy aircraft are anywhere in the area, get rid of external tanks as soon as empty.
4. When in doubt in a dogfight, trade airspeed for altitude.
5. Two good aerial training fights a week are the minimum number necessary to stay in practice. If you aren't fighting the enemy, practice among yourselves.
6. Never continue turning with another aircraft after you are unable to track him with your sight. Pull up immediately and keep your nose behind his tail. If he pulls up, you'll always end up on top because of your attacking airspeed.
7. If, by using speed brakes, you can drift into the radius of turn of the aircraft you are attacking, do it in preference to the YO YO maneuver. It takes less time to get your kill and you don't run the risk of being out-maneuvered by the aircraft you are attacking. What you are leery about is slowing down and thus subjecting yourself to attack. You are at your opponent's airspeed either way and for less time if you use your speed brakes properly. Obviously, the combat area is no place to experiment with this theory. Don't waste your flying time—practice!
8. Cruise at a high Mach.
9. Look around; you can't shoot anything until you see it.
10. Keep the aircraft you are attacking in sight. One glance away is enough to make you kick yourself for ten years.
11. Generally speaking, have an element high and fast when you slow down to maneuver. If you are trying to snip one up in the traffic pattern, you'll find it difficult

at best with all the flak. Don't make the job harder by leaving yourself open for a bounce by the always present enemy CAP flights.

12. Attack from low and behind whenever possible. That's a fighter's poorest visibility area.

13. If you have an enemy aircraft in front, assume there is one behind; there usually is.

14. Know the performance data on all aircraft you are apt to be fighting.

15. Know your "Big Three." Be familiar with glide characteristics, airstart procedures, and fuel consumption at altitude at idle RPM. If you are attacked on the way home, you may need all three to make it back safely.

16. Assume every pilot you meet is the world's best (you can swallow your pride that long) and maneuver your aircraft accordingly until he shows you he is not.

17. Don't shoot unless you're positive it's an enemy aircraft. When it's time to fire you'll know if it's an enemy aircraft or not. If you can't tell, you are out of range.

18. There are three distinct phases in destroying another aircraft in the air:
    a. Maneuvering—85 percent
    b. Positioning the pipper—10 percent
    c. Firing and adjusting the burst—5 percent. Seventy-five percent of all the lost kills are the result of attempting phase (b) and (c) before phase (a) has been adequately solved.

19. Guts will do for skill but not consistently. Know your job in combat or someone else will be flying in your place.

20. Shut up on the radio; if it doesn't concern everyone, get on another channel.

21. Play on the team—no individualists. The quickest way to be an element leader is to be the best wingman in the Squadron.

22. When in doubt—attack!

23. Learn the value and the proper procedure for harmonization.

24. Divide the enemy and conquer. It is very difficult even for the best pilots to work mutual support tactics in high speed jet aircraft. If you can split the tactical formation of the enemy, more often then not his mutual support efforts against you will be ineffective.
25. One last word before you set out to be the next jet ace—*no guts, no glory.* If you are going to shoot him down, you have to get in there and mix it up with him.

Defensive Tactics

We have been discussing the offense almost exclusively. We wish we could tell you that "a good defense will come naturally" or "a good offense is your best defense." Unfortunately, this is not exactly the case, for no matter how good you are there are going to be times when Lady Luck, if no one else, catches up with you. I doubt if there is a single jet ace who can honestly say that he wasn't just plain lucky to get back on at least one mission. "My wingman lost me and didn't say a damn word"; "there were two other aircraft I didn't see"; "my wingman and I transmitted at the same time and I didn't know they were back there"; "I felt just one more burst would do it"; "I didn't think there were any back there"; "I heard him call, 'Break,' but I just had to get him"; "I thought the MiG couldn't turn at low altitude"; "for some reason I thought I was Black Leader and didn't break"; "I saw the long string of 'em but thought I had the last two of the string." These are just a few of the typical comments heard during every debriefing. The line between Ace and POW is a damn thin one at times, not because you aren't good or aren't smart, but because you can't control circumstances. One other reason— let's face it—no matter how good you are, there is another pilot somewhere just a little better.

The basic defensive set-up as described below would be used when aircraft are too low on fuel to fight, have no ammunition, or are damaged to the extent they have lost all their offensive capability.

1. Move your wingman well forward, nearly line abreast.
2. Wingman goes wide when being attacked, so as to present two targets.
3. The aircraft attacked turns away from the other when possible and must then concentrate on the attacker, taking every opportunity to return to homeward heading.
4. The aircraft not attacked watches attacker and turns so as to position himself at six o'clock to the attacker, thus driving him off or shooting him down.
5. If the attack is not pressed, aircraft involved reverse and head for home.
6. If attack is pressed, everything possible should be done by the free aircraft, regarding mutual support turns, to break up the attack.
7. The aircraft attacked breaks hard into the attack, causing attacker to overshoot; if he does not overshoot, there is no choice but to use the diving spiral maneuver hoping the other aircraft will help out. Watch yourself for you may need the "Last Ditch Maneuver" on this one.

The Last Ditch Maneuver

When the diving spiral doesn't do the trick, your last hope is in the "last ditch" maneuver. A good wingman should have one good "last ditch" maneuver and practice it frequently. Keep in mind, though, that it is a "last ditch" maneuver and not one to be used merely because enemy aircraft are somewhere behind you. This maneuver would be used only if an enemy aircraft were at six o'clock to you, in range and firing, or about to fire, and at your airspeed. If he is faster or slower than you, there are obviously other more productive methods of dislodging him from the six o'clock position. If, however, through your own carelessness or inability, you find yourself with an aggressive enemy fighter pilot at six o'clock *and close to your airspeed,* you are going to have a good one to tell the boys at the bar that night—if you get back. Whether or not you do get back will depend a great deal on how much thought and practice you have put in on this last ditch maneuver and also, on how well you fight off the tendency to panic in such a situation. There may be other ways to dislodge an aircraft from the six o'clock position, but the one described here is the best for our money once he is in range and at your airspeed at six o'clock.

1. Get your aircraft into a 5 or 6 G turn as quickly as possible.

2. As your airspeed drops off, lower the nose so you can continue to pull the high Gs.

3. Five or ten thousand feet of this may be enough to lose a pilot who is unsure of himself or half-hearted in his attempt to destroy your aircraft. If he is a good aggressive pilot, however, the fight has just begun.

4. At about 15,000 ft. you are going to have to decide on a "do or die" effort to shake him. Increase you G forces to 6 or 7 Gs, if you can, and slowly reduce throttle to idle.

5. As you reach idle, throw out speed brakes and reverse your direction of turn without easing up on the G forces. (You can do this easily merely by pulling the nose up and over into a high G barrel roll opposite your original direction of turn.)

6. After about thirty degrees of this turn, reverse your turn again. This should not prove too hazardous, for by now you should have your attacker in a full scissor maneuver.

7. As he sees your speed brakes go out, he probably will instinctively throw his out, but he has not yet noticed the decreased throttle setting. Even a good pilot usually will not recognize the initial decrease in throttle because the increase in G forces keeps the two aircraft about the same distance apart. By doing this, you have created the one thing always sought by the defender in any dogfight—lateral separation.

8. After your first turn reversal just play the situation by ear. Keep turning into him and you will find his slightly excessive airspeed will carry him out in front of you. As this happens, he will be forced to break out into some maneuver of his own.
9. Speed brakes "in" and throttle forward immediately as he slides by and you will find yourself in perfect offensive position for a kill.
10. If, for any reason, you don't manage to scissor him through the use of this maneuver, and end up still in front with speed brakes out and throttle back, the pilot behind you will solve any other problems you might have.

Defensive Tactics (Specific)

Now let's get into some standard actions that you'll be expected to perform from time to time. Knowledge dispels fear —know your job and coolly do what is required according to the circumstances.

1. ONE ATTACKED BY TWO: Don't panic no matter how many aircraft are attacking. Panic is your most formidable enemy. As the two come in on you, go to a hundred percent and nose down to pick up a high Mach. As they near the 3,500-2,500 ft. range (range actually should depend on what kind of ammo is being fired at you), break sharply into the attack and make sure you offer no less than a fifty or sixty degree angle off shot at five to six Gs. At this stage of the attack you should see both leader and wingman sliding to the outside of the turn or, if they choose to YO YO, climbing steeply to your rear. Your best move, if they are attempting to turn with you, is to wait until they slide through the trail position then reverse, possibly chopping power and using speed brakes, if required, to get to the rear of the enemy number two man. Base all your maneuvers on the wingman as long as he is still attempting to fly wing. Don't get yourself sandwiched in between the two of them accidentally. If they

decide to YO YO on you and pull up as you begin out turning them, put your aircraft into a diving turn and keep going away from them. With them going up and you going down initially, you'll probably get enough of a range spread to keep you out of trouble. *Don't try to pull up with them if they quit tracking and begin an early pullup*. You haven't as much airspeed and consequently will end up either low or stalled out. Either way you are in worse shape than if you break away and down and do barrel rolls toward the ground while you are picking up speed.

2. ONE ATTACKED BY FOUR: You have a real problem if the four have any idea about what they are doing. Your procedure is to turn into all attacks and to be sure you don't get cocky and try a reverse with the other element spaced about ten seconds behind. Keep both pairs in sight at all times. You'll notice after the first attack or two that the attacking elements are not evenly spaced. Watch for this and, just after turning into the last element, continue your turn and go away at 180 degrees and with all the airspeed you can pick up. Get your nose down quickly, for the gap you are trying to create will depend on your picking up maximum speed as quickly as possible. Each time you turn into an attacker, lower the nose and keep airspeed up. This will keep you ready for an immediate reversal if you should need it. Remember, airspeed is your salvation. Keep your attackers at high angles off, and *DON'T PANIC*. Watch for your chance to break away and down, then get out. Come back tomorrow with a full flight.

3. TWO ATTACKED BY ONE: If you have a good wingman, this should prove no more difficult than if you were a single. Turn into the attack and attempt to swing him outside your turn. Reverse and scissor until you get him to break away and down. If he is extremely sharp and gets in behind you at six o'clock and at your airspeed, during the initial maneuvering phase, spread out and force him to pick one of you or the other. This should be done when he reached the 2,500-3,000 ft. range. The free pilot helps the other one. A tip for the pilot who is attacked—forget about everything but shaking the man behind you. Just hope for the other member of the ele-

ment's help, but make no turns to get it. Keep your eye on
that attacker; keep him at a high angle off, and keep five or
six Gs on the aircraft. Be prepared, if he follows you all the
way down, to use your "last ditch" maneuver.

If the leader and the attacker become entangled in a low
speed scissor maneuver, the wingman may find the opportunity to slide out away from them both. If so, he should do it,
then get his airspeed up and circle the fight, ready to jump the
enemy aircraft in case he should get an advantage on the
leader.

4. TWO ATTACKED BY TWO: Turn into the attackers when
they are just outside firing range (2,500-3,500 ft.) Fight as
though you were as single until you either get an advantage or
until they get one on you. Handle the reverse the same as in
other cases; if they are down on your level trying to turn,
reverse and scissor them as they slide past the trail position. If
they pull up early, as they do in most cases, they probably
won't drift out of your radius of turn far enough to make a
reverse anything but dangerous. As they go up, you go down
—barrel rolls going down to be sure a lucky hit doesn't get
you or your wingman before you can get some distance between yourself and the attackers. If the two of them do make
the turn and you end up with them at your airspeed at six
o'clock, spread out and see what they do. If they stay together
and attack one of you, the other can swing back in, sandwiching them between you and your wingman. The lead (or one
taken) again is on his own, while the free one does his best to
help. If, as you spread out, one of them slides out so each of
you has an attacker, you are in a bad way. This situation calls
for about the only advisable intentional split of element. Each
of you must forget the other and do whatever is necessary to
shake your attacker. If one gets free, naturally, attempt to help
the other. This one's a rough go.

5. TWO ATTACKED BY FOUR: Turn into the attacking lead
element keeping them, as in other attacks, at a high angle off.
Even if they stay low and try to turn with you, be careful
about reversing unless you are sure the second element is still
high above. Frequently, the second element will come in at

about a seven-second interval, in which case a reverse on the lead element could be disastrous. Keep your airspeed up by diving as you turn into each attack and attempt to catch one element in a reverse when the other is too poorly positioned to help out. If they work their way behind you at your airspeed, you may have to try to spread out, hoping that the attacking element will remain intact. If so, the free pilot helps the other. Here he must be particularly careful, for there is the other element to reckon with. In addition to the attackers he is fighting at close range. We must know the whereabouts of the extra element. This is a good situation out of which to break, if possible—especially if attackers know what they are doing. Watch for your chance—it comes with unequal spacing between attacks. Turn into the attack and leave away and down at 180 degrees to your attacker.

6. FOUR ATTACKED BY ONE: By now we begin to see the patterns of defense repeat themselves. The element attacked stays wide and at the last moment breaks away from the other element. The free element plays his supporting action, so as to sandwich the attacker between elements. This forces a trade of aircraft or causes the attacker to reverse into the supporting element, thus freeing the one originally attacked. Be careful not to commit yourself too quickly or too completely. Don't break too early and find you have allowed the attacker to switch targets. If the top friendly element is attacked, he will have better luck breaking down and away from the lead friendly element, calling him and advising him of this as he does it. The leader can delay momentarily, then wheel about, sandwiching the attacker in between. The lead friendly element should arrive for support at such a time as to parry the attack at a range of 2,000 or 3,000 ft. If an advantage is gained on the attacked, the second friendly element should continue to press the attack even if it means separating from the lead element. If it looks questionable, the second element repositions itself as cover for the lead element.

7. FOUR ATTACKED BY TWO: The defense here is exactly as it would be if attacked by a single. If the attacker's wingman is separated for any reason, the free friendly element

should attempt to engage him immediately, keeping him from lucking into a position of advantage as the friendly element maneuvers with the leader of the attack.

8. FOUR ATTACKED BY FOUR: This represents quite a problem for both attacker and the flight being attacked. Assuming the attack is on the high element and is discovered normally, the friendly second element should nose down to pick up speed, calling out the bandits to the flight leader as he does so. From now on the element merely stays wide and waits for the opportune moment to turn hard into the attack. If the second friendly element has reached a position abreast of the lead friendly element, he should, if at all possible, turn away from that element as long as doing so does not give the attackers any advantage. If in doubt, however, always turn into the attack. The second element must be very careful not to break too soon for this is exactly what the attacker desires. If the attacker can make the second element (friendly) think he is going to take them to the deck, and make them dive away, he will switch his attack to the lead element who will then have no chance for help. Should the attack be on the high element and from the side the lead element is on, an early turn into the attack is suggested so that the mutual support can be accomplished easier. If the attack is from the outside of the formation and a turn away from the lead element is assured, delay a little, dropping down before wheeling into the attack. With this procedure it will be a simple matter for the lead element to sandwich the attacker in between. At this stage the lead friendly element must watch carefully the second enemy element. They may commit themselves with a seven or ten second interval behind the lead element or they may still be high above waiting for an opportune time to drop in at six o'clock to another element or single aircraft. Either way, much emphasis must be placed on looking around, for the attackers will have the trump card.

If the initial attack is on the lead element, the second element should come down immediately and attempt to parry the attack. If the attack is broken up, the second friendly element should continue to follow up any advantages gained by pressing home the attack on the first enemy element. Look around!

Don't let the other element surprise you. A call will be necessary to advise the lead element that they are clear at present but on their own from this time on. The fight must be "played by ear" from this point, utilizing the basic principles of offense or defense as the situation may dictate.

Basic Principles of Defense

1. If you slow down, have an element high and fast for support.
2. Except at extreme ranges, always turn into the attack.
3. If there are enemy aircraft anywhere in the area, get rid of external tanks and get your Mach up. It's too late after you spot him.
4. Keep your attacker at a high angle off.
5. Keep airspeeds up when patrolling.
6. Don't ever reverse a turn unless you have your attacker sliding to the outside of the radius of your turn.
7. If you have a "hung" external tank, leave the combat area.
8. If you lose your wingman, both of you should leave the combat area.
9. Know the low speed characteristics of your aircraft. If you are fighting aggressive pilots, you'll need all the know-how you can lay your hands on.
10. Have a "last ditch" maneuver and practice it.
11. Keep a close check on your fuel.
12. "Best defense is a good offense" is good most of the time, but know your defensive tactics.
13. Don't play Russian Roulette! When you're told to "Break"—do it!
14. Avoid staring at contrails or the only aircraft in sight. There are a dozen around for every one you can see.
15. Watch the sun—a well planned attack will come out of the sun when possible.
16. The object of any mutual support maneuver is to sandwich the attacker in between the defending aircraft.

17. In any dogfight, the objective for the defender should be lateral separation. When this is achieved, a reverse and a series of scissors will, if properly executed, put your attacker out in front. The rest is up to you.
18. Place yourself in your attacker's shoes. How would you like to find an enemy flight positioned? Be smart and avoid this formation for your flight.
19. Don't panic; panic is your most formidable enemy!

Employment of Fighters

There were two general methods used to employ jet air-to-air fighters on Fighter Sweep Missions in Korea:

1. Mass formations.
2. Area saturation.

Each method has advantages and disadvantages but either may be needed from one day to the next depending on several factors.

1. Formation the enemy is using.
2. Size of the area you are attempting to control.
3. Performance characteristics of enemy aircraft to be encountered.
4. Quality of enemy pilots.
5. Mission.
6. Supply support available.
7. Evaluation of past tactics in that area.

The Area Saturation Method was used very effectively in Korea because the enemy here in most cases had to be sought out. A successful mission to the enemy was to penetrate fifty or sixty miles into North Korea and then turn and flee for the border. To arrive safely was, apparently, the objective—not to destroy United Nations' aircraft.

In order to trap the enemy aircraft that were penetrating east and south of the Yalu River boundary, our fighters were used in elements of two at varied altitudes in predesignated areas. Our aircraft maintained their vigil until a call was received that MiGs were coming across the river. At this time, those fighters that could converged on the "hot" area allowing us to mass our strength and fight with twice as many independently operating flights (although of two ships instead of four). For the particular situation in Korea, the area saturation proved more effective, for the quality of enemy pilots was generally low; the area we were attempting to control was relatively small; and the aircraft involved were close enough in performance to allow pilot training and individual aggressiveness to be the deciding factors.

Mass formations were conducted by massing two or three squadrons all under one Group Leader; in general, they:

1. Required too much formation flying. Potential leaders were using valuable time flying formation that could have been devoted to looking offensively.
2. Lost the value of surprise. A large formation can be tracked easily by radar and the pilots usually found they were being attacked rather than being the attackers. This can be expected when encountering enemy aircraft with better high altitude performance characteristics.
3. Were not able to remain long enough in the combat area. Too much fuel wasted joining up, flying formation, etc.
4. Did not allow our pilots to properly use the "aggressiveness" advantage we enjoyed.
5. Allowed the Communist radar installation to track us around until it was time to leave the area, at which time they would commit their fighters.

It should be remembered that these conditions existed under the special circumstances in Korea. Even there, we could have been forced into an overnight change by some radical change in tactics by the enemy.

Selection of Flight and Element Leaders in Combat

This seems only remotely connected to the overall problem, but is actually more important to the average squadron in combat than the type of tactics they decide to use. Our personal opinion on the selection of flight and element leaders is this: when a man's life depends on the brand of leadership displayed in the combat area, he has a right to expect his commander to furnish him with the best leaders available in the organization. As a commander, unless you are extremely fortunate, you can't do this and still have all your personnel lined up by date of rank. Here are a few guides recommended for use in a fighter squadron already operating in combat:

1. Assuming he meets a minimum standard of experience and leadership, give the first opportunity to the ranking man.
2. If you must choose between leadership ability and date of rank, or leadership ability and flying time, by all means select the man who has demonstrated the leadership ability.
3. Advise every man who gets a new job that it is a temporary or trial selection; then let him tell you by his actions whether or not the selection is temporary (three weeks to a month should be plenty of time for a man to show his true colors.)
4. Give a man who is not measuring up ample warning, but be honest enough with the rest of your squadron to remove him if he does not produce the desired result in a reasonable length of time.
5. For determining whether he is measuring up, judge him on these things in this order:
   a. Leadership ability and results in combat.
   b. Aggressiveness.
   c. Flying ability.
   d. Cooperation.
   e. Administrative ability.

All these things obviously would produce an ideal officer in combat. You may not get them all in one man; but if you observe your pilots closely and utilize the quality traits you observe, you'll have a head start on most other organizations when considering combat results, morale, and operating efficiency.

Another thing along this line that is worthy of mention. You may as well face the fact that all of your people will not be as aggressive as you would like. You can count on about three, if you are fortunate, of your pilots in the squadron to possess those things necessary to be exceptional leaders and produce more than an occasional kill or two. There will be a secondary group, both wingmen and element leaders, who want to do the job but don't have the experience yet to do it.

Select Bibliography

Barclay, George, *Angels 22*, William Kimber

Bishop, W. A., *Winged Warfare*, Hodder & Stoughton

Boyington, Gregory, *Baa Baa Black Sheep*, Putnam

Forrester, Larry, *Fly for Your Life*, Frederick Muller

Graham-White, Claude and Harper, Harry, *Heroes of the Flying Corps*, Hodder & Stoughton

Hartney, Harold E., *Wings Over France*, Bailey Bros & Swinfen

Johnson, J. E., *Wing Leader*, Chatto & Windus

Kiernan, R. H., *Captain Albert Ball V.C.*, Aviation Book Club

Lee, Arthur Gould, *No Parachute*, Jarrolds

Lewis, Cecil, *Saggitarius Rising*, Peter Davies

McCudden, James, *Flying Fury*, Aviation Book Club

McLanachan, William, *Fighter Pilot*, Routledge & Kegan Paul

Price, Alfred, *The Hardest Day*, McDonald & Janes

Richtofen, Manfred von and Ulanoff, Stanley M., *The Red Baron*, Bailey Bros & Swinfen

Sakai, Saburo and Caidin, Martin, *Samurai*, William Kimber

Shaw, Robert, *Fighter Combat*, US Naval Institute Press, Annapolis

Udet, Ernst and Ulanoff, Stanley M., *Ace of the Iron Cross*, Arco Publishing

Index

FROM PERSONAL JOURNALS TO BLACKLY HUMOROUS ACCOUNTS

VIETNAM

DISPATCHES, Michael Herr
> 01976-0/$4.50 US/$5.95 Can

"I believe it may be the best personal journal about war, any war, that any writer has ever accomplished."
> —Robert Stone, *Chicago Tribune*

A WORLD OF HURT, Bo Hathaway
> 69567-7/$3.50 US/$4.50 Can

"War through the eyes of two young soldiers...a painful experience, and an ultimately exhilarating one."
> —*Philadelphia Inquirer*

ONE BUGLE, NO DRUMS, Charles Durden
> 69260-0/$3.95 US/$4.95 Can

"The funniest, ghastliest military scenes put to paper since Joseph Heller wrote *Catch-22*"
> —*Newsweek*

AMERICAN BOYS, Steven Phillip Smith
> 67934-5/$4.50 US/$5.95 Can

"The best novel I've come across on the war in Vietnam"
> —Norman Mailer